DOO-WOP! and THE G-CLEFS

The saga of America's last original Doo-Wop group from the 1950s still performing.

By Michael Devlin

Copyright 2014 Michael G. Devlin

All rights reserved. No part of this book may be reproduced, stored in a retrieve system, or transmitted by any means, electronic, mechanical, photo copying, recording, or otherwise, without written permission from the author.

Special thanks to photographer's Allan E. Dines (North Star Photography-Wayland, Massachusetts), and Jean Hangarter (South Boston) for their individual contribution assisting me in telling this story. - Michael G. Devlin

Thanks to Debbi Stocco of MyBookDesigner.com for her and her company's expertise and commitment with the editing and process of my manuscript being transposed into book form. My gratitude for her professional guidance along with her company's knowledge which was the necessary link for the success of my story to be heard. Much appreciated. - Michael G. Devlin

ISBN 13: 978-0-9905157-3-9 (print version)
ISBN 13: 978-0-9905157-1-5 (ebook version)

*To my parents for their love, support, and professional guidance.
It wouldn't have been possible without them.*

Table of Contents

Sunday People 7
A Welcomed Return 8
Right Place, Right Time 9
The G-Clefs 11
A Different Direction 17
Starting Out 18
Lots of Papa 22
Bumble Bee Slim 25
Dr Harp 28
Merry Go Round 34
The First Show 40
Shorty's Doo-Wop Show 48
Lombardo's 51
Bill 53
Boston City Hall Plaza 56
Rita 60
Falmouth 64
Beverly Wedding 67
Scullers 68
Jail Time 72
Wonderland 75
Midway Café 79
"Steppin Out" 82
To Bass, or Not to Bass, that is the Question 88
Dick 91
Brutal 92
Looking a Gift Horse in the Mouth 97
Rolls Royce Club 98
Mr. Bob Walker 100
Mt. Un-Pleasant 106
Harlem 112
Rain, Rain, Go Away, Come Back Again Some Other "Mother's Day" 118
The Willows 122
The Web We Weave 125

    The Hatch Shell 128
    Next Stop Pittsburgh 134
    Symphony Hall 137
    Chuck Carbo 140
    Last Gig..141
    Coming Around Full Circle 142
    Invite is not Optional 145

Special Feature 147
    In Their Own Words... 149
    Life on the Road 160

About the Author 173

April 2014

    I worked for the G-Clefs from 1992 until 2002. We did a total of 42 shows over a ten year span which is not a lot, but each show proved to be different from the previous gigs. I had to consider which shows stood out the most so that I could write my book within a reasonable volume just to keep the pace of it interesting.

    A lot of authors who write about Doo-Wop present their publication as a collection of singing groups on a whole because it's the only way to fill a book with factual knowledge. Nobody has written about any one specific Doo-Wop singing group, until now.

    ~ Michael G. Devlin

Sunday People

In 1997 PBS (Public Broadcast System) wanted to commemorate the Fiftieth Anniversary of Doo-Wop on its TV show, for the viewing public to enjoy they put together a show of this never forgotten music.

MANY OF THE ORIGINAL groups were featured including: The Platters; "The Great Pretender"; the Del-Vikings, "Come Go With Me"; Gene Chandler, "Duke of Earl"; Johnny Maestro, "Sixteen Candles"; the Capris, "There's a Moon out Tonight"; the Marcel's, "Blue Moon"; the Jive Five, "My True Story"; the Cadillac's, "Speedo"; the Harptones, "Life Is But a Dream" along with the Channels, the Moonglows, the Flamingos, the Spaniels, the Skyliners, and the Cleftones.

This PBS production was done on a grand scale with professional theater settings, and the prop's needed to round out that 50s decor, to help set the stage for all those singing groups asked to come perform and sing again.

This newly rediscovered music from the 1950s would be back in demand after it was awakened from a restful golden slumber.

The music was exciting and still intact. It was great listening to the harmonic melodies that demonstrated the true capability of what the human voice can produce in unison with their fellow vocalist on stage while adding their own choreography and agility into their act. It was a little bit of flair needed with their natural ability of showmanship that still had a creative side to their routines as we watched and listened.

Their suits (clothes) were matched in a coordinated fashion with one another, fitting with their performance and adding to their presence, leaving us transfixed while watching them perform.

It was sensational and sharp on everybody's part to look and sound as professional now, for the many people who became fans again or were re-acquainted and reconnected with Doo-Wop. Watching this PBS show seemed to me like I was witnessing a reincarnation from that great and wonderful Doo-Wop era. It had transformed all of us back in time and now it was evident that we were about to get another healthy dose of it when it returned from where it started.

It would still have enough life left to it as it filtered its way back into our culture not to be forgotten with the passing of time some fifty years later.

For most of these singing group's they would find that they too would be in demand again singing on stage back out on the professional circuit in music hall's, or concert theater's for live performance's all around the country.

In a very fortunate circumstance for me, I too would be in the thick of that 1990s comeback as well.

A Welcomed Return

THE MUSIC OF DOO-WOP is an original American art form that would catch on with a younger generation in a more compatible and memorable time period in our history known as the "Fabulous 50s".

Doo-Wop would be closely associated with the adolescents of another time that would give a voice to a generation filled with teenager's looking to imitate anything about life through their version of what music would become for them.

We would see it rise from its original birth in the 1950s to hitting its stride once again during the 1970s, then resurface and incredibly find its way, "Back to the Future" during the 1990s. That is very difficult to do, and extremely unusual for any form of music to have a repetitive life in any format involving anything that has to do with popular music.

A true quality product will never fail even after it has proved itself over and over. Anything to do with Doo-Wop would remain resilient because nothing that good could ever outlast itself.

Even after it has proven its own sense of accomplishment, it was obvious that Doo-Wop was not going to fade away to be forgotten like other musical styles that seemed to have vanished and disappeared as a new decade approached changing the public's interest's before Doo-Wop came back to life.

During the 1990s the world took notice when music fans declared that Doo-Wop would be welcomed back knowing that this American home grown product had re-surfaced and found a renewed friendship with the public.

As the future drew itself a little closer to this unforgotten music it remained an influence on what rock 'n roll would eventually become.

Right Place, Right Time

I NEVER IMAGINED THAT I would write a book about the G-Clefs it would have never entered my mind, if it wasn't for my dad. He would always cut out newspaper articles, mostly stories relating to music, such as James Brown "the Godfather of Soul" who seemed to constantly have run-ins with the law there in South Carolina. James Brown always made the local papers with one of his more recent and multiple arrests, so my dad would send me the article.

Or my dad would send me a photograph from the same newspaper showing one of Eric Clapton's guitars being auctioned off for a charity event somewhere. The newspaper article had the complete story along with a pretty good definitive explanation on a note from my dad who would attach it to the article before sending it to me.

My father sent me another one of those music related stories in April 2009 with a human interest story the newspaper wrote on a local guy named, Jim Washok. One of the many jobs "he had in life was working as a roadie" (someone who helps setup, and breaks down the band's equipment). It's back breaking work, and he did that during the 1980s for a "Hair" band by the name T.H. Latona.

"They wanted to make it big," said Washok during the paper's interview with him, "they weren't joking around." T. H. Latona won several "battle of the band" competitions for the "Tri-State" area which included Pennsylvania, Ohio, and New York.

They became so popular, they were asked to open for bigger bands touring in the area including Heart, Cheap Trick, and Ozzy Osbourne.

While he was their roadie, Washok got to meet roadies from bigger bands, but "T.H. Latona broke up before making it big."

Jim Washock

Washok said he helped set up for some of the eras biggest bands, including "Poison", "Winger", "Fleetwood Mac", "Skid Row", and "Aerosmith" among the many other rock bands.

"I've had tons of fights while working backstage," Washok said, "guys wanting to know where their girlfriends were, people wanting autographs during the middle of a set, fights in the parking lots...." With encouragement from his sister, Washok was planning to write a book about his experiences.

I started thinking to myself as I read this article on Washok, that I too have a story that's just as colorful what I went through with my own experience with music.

When I joined the Doo-Wop group that claimed me, it become much bigger than anything I would ever be involved with no matter what happened to me the rest of my life as a musician. I didn't know if I could or couldn't put something together that might be as good as Washok's book, but I was going to try. It might be easier said than done, but I knew I had to make the effort.

As I stared to write my memory began to unfold, and from there I was able to see all of the stories I had in abundance about this exciting, but sometimes excruciating adventure that was mixed with the good and the bad.

I felt it was time to tell the story of the G-Clefs and bring their lives as this singing group returning to the forefront as Doo-Wop, became popular again during the 1990s. But it would be more like putting Frankenstein back together again after he already went on a rampage roaming the local village scaring the poor peasant's and farmer's, who were doing nothing but tending to their own lives as simple folk, half to death.

Maybe I'd be the one responsible for putting it all back together only to unleash it again into the public domain and creating another panic. I don't know, but I had to try if I were to ever find out. It was still an opportunity that came my way by default, although there was a certain level of luck that had a lot to do with it. But it still came down to being in the "Right place at the Right time."

The G-Clefs

The G-Clefs 1956

DURING THE 1950S SOME GROUPS only lasted as long as their "one hit wonder" song would last on the charts and were never heard from again. Still many others if they had a hit on Billboard's 100 would help propel that group for a lifetime.

Because of their "one hit wonder" song, they would be in demand on the Doo-Wop oldies circuit making live appearances and performing on shows. There were hundreds of Doo-Wop singing group's that started out and recorded during the 1950s, but only a handful would last a lifetime. Unfortunately the groups that did last a little longer would have to periodically replace one of their original members who may have died so that the group could continue to sing and give a live performance somewhere.

When Doo-Wop returned during the 1990s it didn't deny anything towards these singing groups. Their music would return them to the present as they continued to be part of their legacy-that they were responsible for. It was their recorded heritage that initiated the early stages of what Rock 'n Roll had started out to be.

Over the course of time as with everything in life, there would only be three remaining singing group's left who still remained intact with their original members. They were, the "Four Tops", the "Dells", and the "G-Clefs". The Dells would have a hit in 1956 called "Oh What a Night" which peaked in the top five in the R&B charts, but when an original member of the Dells, Johnny Funches, had died in January 1998, along with Levi Stubbs of the "Four Tops" who died in October 2008, that would leave the G-Clefs "as the last remaining Doo-Wop singing group with its original line-up from when they first started out during the 1950s."

Since 2008, the G-Clefs have truly stood alone with this unique distinction, and would be Doo-Wop's remaining original group that stood the test of time.

The G-Clefs recording 1957

The G-Clefs career began during the 1950s and it propelled them into a world where they sampled stardom that was truly meant for them to experience as singers. They too would make another effort to return to show business when Doo-Wop called their name, as they would now be included among the many singing groups from that honor roll of 1950s vocal harmonizers.

The G-Clefs had returned hoping to sing another day as they were graciously given another chance to do so. They also saw another opportunity where they felt the most comfortable, on stage in front of an audience.

I saw the G-Clefs work hard at singing and entertaining crowds from small private functions to large public events. It made me realize just how big another part of their music meant to people.

Through the G-Clefs I met people who truly believed in Doo-Wop and practically lived for it. It would leave an impression on me as to how much Doo-Wop was such a vital part to their lives.

The G-Clefs

Although I had a very limited knowledge of Doo-Wop, I was welcomed to be among the multitude of friend's they had collected over the years I became part of their extended family of other Doo-Woppers, and there would be lots of them.

In the end, it was me that become part of their world as it eclipsed any other thought's I would have about my future as a guitar player, and that maybe I should be somewhere else other than this new world I found myself in.

To me I thought they were just some forgotten group of Doo-Wop singer's whose name was buried at the bottom of music's previous journey a long time ago.

I got to live and experience a different style of music that allowed me to meet people who made their living as famous entertainers. I would share the same stage with Ruth Brown, Ertha Kitt, the Righteous Brothers, Gregory Hynes, Bill Haley's original Comets, Shirley Reeves from the Shirelles, and the wonderful Ms. Lavern Baker.

My band would be the supporting musicians for notable's such as Bobby Lewis, "Tossing & Turning"; Bobby Taylor of the Visounts; the Willows; Chuck Carbo and the Spiders; the Dub's; and the Vocaleer's.

I was to gain another perspective to what I was now involved with, but this time I was inside looking out, seeing another angle that only the G-Clefs had with their own music.

Working for the G-Clefs proved to be unpredictable with every turn I took with them. It could be very unforgiving at times with this "Baptism by Fire" that seemed to be the only method I was allowed to work with, even as good and solid business circumstance's presented themselves, only resulting in near failure's along the way.

I would experience the ups and downs when I witnessed how professional they were as they

"Hit" the stage. But off stage was another story to their lives. Their music would demand the most out of me, challenge me some more, and put me in some very tough and precarious situations before we got anywhere near the success that I thought we deserved.

When I realized it was my place to be as their band leader, I started to get a little more immersed with the G-Clefs. Whatever responsibilities I had would allow me to go beyond being just one of the many musicians that came and went out of their lives.

I also knew it was going to be different than anything else as they expected me to keep it all together for another oldies show we were scheduled to play somewhere close to our home town of Boston.

The G-Clefs were good, but as a whole they were a handful. It would be more than what I could handle at times, and it was definitely different than what I expected from any one of them. They knew how to entertain, and sometimes they did that in un-peculiar and unconventional way's, but nobody will ever get to work with the G-Clefs as closely as I did it was me and my band, playing the music from another generation that we happen to love, share and do what we had to do for this un-known "Cinderella" Doo-Wop group from Boston called the G-Clefs.

Mike Devlin

A Different Direction

THE WORLD OF DOO-WOP had figured out exactly where I was and made its way right into the middle of my very busy life. It picked me out of the bunch, and put me down into the center of that 50s Doo-Wop revival just as it was about to sweep the entire country for a "Third" time, making unprecedented musical history in the process.

This kind of music was not something I initially wanted to do, but it seemed that it was decided for me as it allowed me and my band to be the warm bodies needed if the G-Clefs stood a chance for another grab at stardom, as it approached their lives once more.

I would be pressed into service to find and fill that void that had come due to them. They would depend on me to salvage what was left of their career, help get it back on track, and pull it together with what was left of them being the professional entertainers they once were.

In essence I would be the all-important link that was needed to help forge their music back together as they returned to the limelight, they once enjoyed as a singing group from years before.

I accepted my fate and would take on the responsibility as their conscientious band leader if I had to fire a musician or if I needed to find a substitute to fill in for one of our live shows somewhere.

I could be the equipment man or a roadie moving heavy equipment back and forth. I scheduled rehearsals or did any of the introductions, made the necessary announcements at weddings, or mc'd any other shows, but there was one job I truly despised, and more or less hated.

It's what I called being their "REFEREE"the guy who had to get in the middle of the G-Clefs themselves when it seemed that they were about to kill one another over harsh words that would easily lead to an argument that quickly got out of hand.

It consisted mostly of just breaking up a small disagreement that got started at the drop of a hat, but if I didn't do that, it would easily escalate into a full blown physical squabble between any one of them at a moment's notice.

I was forced to learn to think on my feet in the heat of the moment, and act quickly toward the problems that seemed to accompany the G-Clefs and their different personalities. I did my best to cope and deal with them under any of the circumstances that presented itself to me, but I also didn't want the responsibility of being judge and jury to somebody else's life either.

It wasn't possible for me to predict the role I would end up playing within the G-Clefs, but this added responsibility of wearing the many hats made it all necessary to hold it together just to kept any amount of stability to the soon to be chaos that always needed my attention.

I knew I would be foolish to try and change anything about their behavior, but I had to keep some form of civil order before our small ship sank before it was given a chance to set sail. I was committed, but not foolish enough to intently drown myself in the process of trying to help them. I could not anticipate that the musical journey offered to me would turn into one of the roughest roller coaster rides in any amusement park on planet earth.

I was also about to find out that that roller coaster I got onto would belong to the G-Clefs themselves.

Starting Out

IN HIGH SCHOOL I BELONGED to a couple of garage rock bands, but soon lost interest as I went into my college years. I was still living at home, studying and working a part time job pumping gas down the street.

After I graduated from college I started working as an expeditor for a small company. At that time I also discovered computers as a new trend towards working somewhere as a professional employee and I knew the pay would be better for me. But I would have to go to school at night to complete courses in computer science.

When I graduated I received a job offer from MIT. I was a computer operator working inside of their huge computer room, crammed with very large floor model computers and printers. I would monitor what information that had to be complied, along with the data that needed to be retrieved for the engineers who worked there.

This was an "Entry" level job, with an "Entry" level pay, and it was pretty clear once I started working there that I needed to make some extra money doing anything to improve my situation. I needed a part time job, pumping gas or washing dishes, anything that would help me make ends meet. My other option was to take that electric guitar I kept from my high school days and join some blues bar band somewhere and play on the weekends. Then I could take that fifty dollars I'd earned, and use it for my weekly gas and food money.

Incredible now, but that's what I did. I basically lived off the money I earned playing gigs and took my paycheck from my job, eventually to pay off my (computer) school loan, and credit card debt.

Although I had some working knowledge of the guitar, that knowledge would be considered rudimentary. I did have the basic understanding, but I would have to start all over from the beginning learning how to play the guitar beyond the simple scales and chords that everybody has to know before they move on to reach the next level of skill.

It would prove to be tough for somebody like me, but time was on my side. I had to get busy with what was made available for me to learn. I decided to go hang out and hit one of the many jam sessions around town, but I needed to find a place where those real guitar players knew what they were doing so I could watch and learn.

I would eventually discover a place called the "Cantab Lounge", and started hanging out there on Sunday night's for their R&B (rhythm and blues) jam session.

The Cantab

The Cantab Lounge is a lively entertainment club with an old style elongated bar that stretches on forever. It has a small stage with tables and chairs for about 200 people to sit and enjoy the music that's played there on the weekends.

Located in Central Square Cambridge, the "Cantab" was not too far from where I rented a room in a house, and where I worked during the day. It was a perfect location, and it would serve me well as time started to happen for my quest to become this guitar player that I felt I needed to be. I've always believed that there had to be an objective to what I was doing if I wanted to play like a pro, and I also knew that there had to be some kind of promise to it if I were to stay with it. I would not be disappointed with either one of those aspiring thoughts, not what-so-ever.

I had no expectations about playing guitar on stage, but perception from any distance can be deceptive no matter how close or far away you are from it. It started to become a dream come true for me with the little amount of success I was experiencing.

It wouldn't take long before any thought of being a musician would pale in comparison to the reality of the music business; proving how difficult it really was working within its parameter's. Not only do you have to have the incentive to want to play music, but you had to be flexible toward the things that would challenge you with what you were supposed to be doing as a musician.

I knew that this was a very different world because of the late night hours and sometimes the long distances I drove to get to some smoky bar somewhere in the middle of nowhere to do a gig. I also knew about the druggies, and the drugs that would be offered to me if I desired to indulge myself in their small pile of cocaine sitting on top of their cocktail table as their girlfriend looked on. It was mine for the taking, and of course there were the alcoholics always looking to me to buy them a drink because they didn't have any money. Or there were the women in the clubs with their husbands (which didn't stop them from), asking me for a date. It certainly wasn't the most memorable side, but rather the reality of being out there playing.

I didn't let it bother me too much. I knew I had enough self-discipline to work in that environment. More importantly, I wanted to cut it as a guitar player and from there I could get around whatever obstacles that invariably came my way.

I had three simple but short rules I would live by: "no drugs"; "no excessive drinking"; and be careful of the "girls", regardless if their boyfriends or husbands were in the club that night. Not that I didn't take advantage of that situation once in a while, but I did prefer if they were single and only then was it somewhat tempting for me. But I always found a reason to walk away from a situation that could possibly turn out bad for the both of us. A jealous boyfriend is not something you really want to tangle with, besides it was more important for me to get through the night so that I could make the next gig in one piece.

I anticipated the stereotypes of musicians and entertainers I would come across, and I would not be disappointed. I learned to recognize the character of different singers I worked for, whether they sang Blues, Rock 'n Roll or anything Motown.

Some of those people completely depended on what work they could get as an entertainer. I met singers who were out there striving to do, by whatever means possible, to be recognized as the true talent they thought they were; sometimes injecting a taste of their own fantasies if they thought it would get them any closer to stardom.

Their egos had a profound effect on their better judgment, but sometimes it was all they had to keep themselves going. It was that kind of behavior that I would witness, and I'd see it play itself out over and over during the course of me being their back-up guitarist.

I would also see some of these people completely stop short of any real success that came their way. You don't get too many opportunities in this business, and when you do, you try not to let it slip through your fingers. For whatever reason, they didn't seem to have a grasp or any mechanical ability to understand another crucial part of being in the music business: to try and succeed, and do the best of your ability, so you can have the financial rewards and freedom that comes along with it.

Very simply, try to go further than where you are at the moment; advancing your skills as an entertainer for people who might enjoy what you do with your music. If they appreciate what you are doing as an artist, then you'll be given some small chance that could propel you to a much more meaningful career.

I've seen singers and musicians that think of themselves as more of a spectator than an entertainer, and that's the dividing line between those that succeed, and those who end up failing. In the end it was more often than not, where I would see most of them fail. You either party or play, you can't do both.

My equipment was mediocre at best as I stared out. I borrowed a Peavey amp from Brian Pecto one of the guys I worked with, and I had my '76 Fender Strat that froze on me one night as I drove down to Cape Cod to do a gig. It was a subzero winter night when I left Boston and that guitar was in the trunk of my car for the two hour drive.

When I got inside that toasty warm club, the finish on my Strat cracked, and the neck stared going berserk, the steel truss rod inside the neck kept warping and bending as it tried to thaw itself out. I wrestled all night long trying to keep that thing in tune.

That guitar, which I kept from all the years before, did not rest sitting in my closet. It would take me places I knew existed, but I certainly didn't plan on going there, at least without any apprehension as to what I was getting myself involved with. All I wanted to know was what my worth would be if I became "that" guitar player and how far I could take it.

I certainly had little or no expectations or any grandeur about being a rock star or anything close that might resemble a goal that some people have. My trusty guitar would lead me through a series of well-established musical styles before I finally reached the door steps of Doo-Wop.

Lots of Papa

IT WAS TALENT NIGHT at the Cantab, and I had just gotten off stage when I was approached by a slender black man named Tee.

"Yo man, you's good brother, you's really good," he said. "Oh thanks," I responded to him as if he didn't say anything to me. I didn't completely ignore him I just thought he was being polite along with some small encouragement on his part.

People would say things like that to me knowing I was new at this, so I simply didn't take notice of it right away with what I thought was a compliment. Tee continued to focus on having a conversation with me when he asked me, "Can you's fill's in for my's 'Gitar player next week, he be out of town, and I needs somebodys to fill's in for him."

I was somewhat flattered that anybody thought I was good enough to substitute for their absent 'Gitar player, but I really hadn't been playing that long, so at first I didn't quite understand why he wanted me to fill in on guitar for him.

If it was clear to me that I was still somewhat a novice at this, then how come he didn't see it too? It didn't make sense to me, but it would have to be a quick decision on my part. I didn't want to let any opportunity and maybe the only one, pass me by that night.

I thought to myself, "alright, let me see were this is going, maybe it'll be something good for this new chosen path of wanting to be a working musician." I turned to Tee and asked him, "What kind of songs do you guys play?" Without hesitation he said, "My Girl" by the Temp's, and other songs by Diana Ross and the Sue-preems."

A lot of musicians in the Cantab grew up on that Rhythm & Blues music and it seemed so effortless for them to just play that stuff. It would amaze me as I sat there, and studied what they were doing every Sunday night. But I was far removed from playing any of that stuff live, never mind working it out in a club setting where Tee expected me to plug in and play it automatically.

I admitted to Tee I didn't know that R&B stuff, but he said, "No problems man, you's come's to the house, I show you man."

When he said that I began to think, wow he was pretty confident with what he saw in me, so I told him, "Yeah, alright, I'll come over." I had an idea how these songs went, but now I was gonna have help in learning those R&B songs for the club work that had now called on me that would start my career as a working guitar player.

It turned out that Tee was the Bass player for "Lots of Papa & the Fabulous Flames", a club act which featured an out front singer named "Lots-of-Papa". The band primarily played the Black club circuit in and around Boston, and as far south as Hartford, Connecticut and in between.

"Lots-of-Papa" was a big robust of a man and a very conscientious dresser who liked to wear his fine jewelry along with his distinguishable gold watch that he always had to wear no matter what it wasn't over the top flashy with all that he was wearing, but classy.

The band played all the songs they were doing at the Cantab like, "When Something is Wrong with my Baby" and, "I'm a Soul Man", by Sam and Dave, "In the Midnight Hour" by Otis Redding, and "I Feel Good" by James Brown. Again, this would be a real step up for me, plus somebody taking the time to actually show me what I needed to know. This only fueled my desire to see that I was being taken seriously now.

After going to Tee's house for a couple of lessons, I was able to hone in a little bit on the music he wanted me to play but it still wasn't enough time for me to get a solid grasp to any of it. Then the reality of it hit me, I would have to learn the songs on the gig itself, and that's a tuff way to learn any song out there, especially if it has multiple chord changes, and these songs had plenty.

At first I laid low playing what I could with the "Fabulous Flames" until my confidence caught up with me. It was a matter of repetition that I would eventually understand the chords and the progressions involved with the music. I was starting to understand how those songs were structured, but with me being the new addition to the band, they expected me to pull my weight. I was already getting the hang of it, but it was the keyboard and Bass player who helped push me along. They carried the band, and were patient with me until I could get up to speed with the rest of the group. I thought that was pretty cool for those guys to be patient with me like that.

For what I thought would be a temporary short stay with "Lots of Papa and the Fabulous Flames", this had now changed. I was told their guitarist was actually leaving their group altogether. I'm guessing I was the closest warm body who happened to be the only guitar player available for Tee to grab a hold of that night when he introduced himself to me at the Cantab

I wasn't upset or anything, but to begin with I certainly felt like a fish out of water with this music and there's nothing worse than feeling any ounce of inadequacy, especially if you don't have a full understanding of anything you're involved with.

I was always grateful to catch a ride to the gigs with Frank, our keyboard player, and once I loaded my equipment into his van we'd head out. I liked riding with Frank because he had a great sound system, and he always had some really good "funky" music from the Gap Band, and Sly and the Family Stone. That stuff just sounded great, and again another eye opener for me. That kind of music had a little more edge than what we were playing in the clubs with "Lot's-of-Papa".

Not that it really mattered to me, but one night Frank decided to tell me that "Lots of Papa" was not allowed to ride in his van. "Really?" I said as we were driving back to Boston after doing another late night gig somewhere.

"Yeah," he said, "Lots-of-Papa" broke my running board when he stepped on it to get in my van." He was that heavy of a person, the running board snapped right off of Frank's van, it just couldn't hold "Lots-of-Papa's" weight.

"After that," Frank said, "I wouldn't let him ride in my van no more. I told's 'Lots of Papa', man you gut's to find's your own way's to the gigs."

"Wow," I said, "I don't blame you."

We started moving pretty fast, going from Boston, to Providence, Rhode Island then over to Hartford, Connecticut, and then back to Boston playing gigs. Funny, but at the time I started to realize that there was this whole other circuit of "Black" clubs that existed between these metropolitan cities. It was almost like an underground venue for black people to go, and enjoy their own preference, and style of music.

It was just another world that opened up to me that I had no idea even existed. It also began to sink in that this was probably the Northern version of the "Chitlin Circuit" we were working. This is where I saw that food was also part of these club goers culture as they joined their friend's for a couple of drinks, dance to our music, sit and relax eating some homemade cooking (southern style) on a Saturday night.

After about a year of working for "Lots-of-Papa", I decided to tell him that I was leaving the band. Before I could finish my sentence he said, "We have a New Year's Eve gig at the Holiday Inn down in Providence, Rhode Island, can you do one more show for us."

I said, "Yeah sure, why not, it shouldn't be a problem."

He said, "Meet me at my house, you catch a ride with me and my sister to the gig." When I got to his house, I put my guitar and amp in the trunk of his Fleetwood Cadillac, jumped into the back seat, and was ready to do one last show with "Lots of Papa and the Fabulous Flames".

I was enjoying the peaceful ride until "Lots-of-Papa" started to turn off at the next exit ramp to get onto the other side of on the highway.

I said, "Lots-of-Papa, what are you doing man?!"

He said, "We have to go back to Boston, I forgot my gold watch, you know the one I always wear on the shows."

We were already half way to Providence, so I said, "...your watch, can't you do the show without your watch?"

"Oh no," he said, "people's need to see my watch when I hold up the microphone to sing."

Wow, that was pure vanity, and what I thought was unreasonable at the time, but again it would only impress upon me another important part of show business whatever image you portray to an audience is just as important as the music you intend to play for them. Your image is worth just as much as the entertainment itself.

I learned as much as I possibly could with their group, but more importantly what it took to play in a show band. My experience as a musician with "Lots of Papa" had seasoned me as a guitarist. The skill's I learned would prove to be an asset for me when I would rely on them to get me through the more challenging problems I would face later on. It would prove to be nothing more than a "dress rehearsal" for my future involvement with Doo-Wop when the demand for it would come back around with an added velocity that would bring it to the forefront of popular music.

I was subconsciously ready for its arrival without even realizing it, but right now I just wanted to return back to the Cantab's jam session and hang out with my friends, along with some girls I got to know on those Sunday nights.

Bumble Bee Slim

I RETURNED TO THE CANTAB'S Sunday night jam session where I happened to meet a self-appointed blues singer by the name of Bumble Bee Slim who's sitting at the bar in an unassuming posture with a half filled shot-glass in front of him pretending to be minding his own business.

I didn't know what to make of him at first. He seemed to me to be a loner, someone who more or less had the presence of being a bar room brawler than anything else.

It didn't take long before I realized the only connection the both of us had was the affection we both shared for the : "Blues" and what little talent we both possessed would come to life when we got up on stage that night playing music we were both familiar with.

It also came to light that we were one in the same with this music, but as far as anything else involving our lives, we couldn't have been more opposite than any two people could possibly be. That old saying about "Two Pea's in a Pod" "being the same would be difficult to comprehend at that moment.

Bumble Bee Slim certainly portrayed himself as someone who was familiar with that well-worn dirt road down South somewhere, as just another drifter in the hopes of finding a direct connection to the blues, as he stood alone at the crossroads before midnight waiting for the Devil himself to appear, willing to sell his soul in the belief that Satin would help him gain some small notoriety as a famous blues singer.

I also sensed that music was all Bumble Bee Slim had to his life, and he was willing to share with anybody who might listen to him talk about his exploits as this authentic bluesman.

Bumble Bee Slim

Bumble Bee Slim and me at the Cantab.

Any interest I showed only invited him to exaggerate any one of his adventure's that he'd probably told another stranger like me a dozen times before in another small-time bar full of people enjoying the music being played.

He was as close as anybody I met that was committed to understanding the blues or resembling the authenticity that only another musician like me would have appreciated.

At first it was a bit strange to me as I listened to his exploits about whatever small adventure he had had, whether it was a romantic tryst with a woman a couple of nights before, or a street fight that he got into the night before that.

At the time it amused me more than anything else. I just never met anyone who put himself through that kind of trouble before, and I thought it was a lot of effort and energy for nothing.

What impressed me the most was how flawless he spoke about any one of the blues master's like Howling Wolf or Muddy Waters. Those original blues singers sang about the "Down and Outs", and how hard and sometimes cruel life could be.

I think Bumble Bee Slim associated himself with that way of life probably believing that imitating art or anything associated with those "Down and Outs" would allow him to have the sort of identity, and that we too would recognize him as this bluesman returning from that dusty road somewhere down South after dealing with the Devil himself.

Even though Bumble Bee Slim didn't own a car he relied on other people to get around. He had his pride, but he never turned down someone willing to buy him a drink, nor a breakfast I bought him at an all-night diner after a gig we just got through playing. Once in a while I'd give him a place to sleep (on my couch) because he had no money to stay somewhere else. Then I'd see him walk into the club we were working wearing a brand new pair of $300 boots.

All of his excessive behavior didn't stop me from joining Bumble Bee Slim's blues band playing guitar as close to the version of electric blues that I possibly could so that he could sing his preferred Chicago blues style of music. I also mixed that good ole Rock 'n roll, Chuck Berry stuff which I freely injected just to keep the dancer's happy and to round out the night.

It would be another learning process working as Bumble Bee Slim's much needed sideman. Being a vital member of his band I too started to believe that I had some sort of direct link to this music from the past. It wasn't far away. Nothing is when It's close to your heart like the blues was for me.

For Bumble Bee Slim and me, as opposite as we were in our own lives, it proved how much we were one in the same. Another part of our being became connected when we stepped up on stage back at the Cantab, playing blues together as if we were "Two Pea's in a Pod".

Dr Harp

I PERSONALLY BELIEVE THAT SOME people have no business being in the entertainment field, but I could see it wasn't going to stop this guy from jumping in with both feet first, even if it was at the shallow end of the pool.

In his own mind he was professional enough to be a band leader out front singing and playing harmonica, but of course you also need to have the talent to begin with, and the ability that it takes to be in a Rock 'n roll blues band. It doesn't matter who you are.

After my time with Bumble Bee Slim, I returned to the Cantab so I could feel somewhat at home again, but I was approached by yet another singer looking for a guitar player for a bunch of gigs he lined up for himself down on Cape Cod.

I noticed this guy wearing a tan "Indiana Jones" style hat along with snakeskin boots and a leather vest, who approached me. I decided to give him a little more attention than I normally would with anybody else.

"Hi, I'm Dr Haaap," he said as he introduced himself.

I replied, "What? Dr Happ?"

"No. Dr Haaap," he repeated.

"Oh," I said, "you mean Harp like in Harpsichord."

"Yeah," he replied, "that's what I said, Dr Haaap."

He has a thick Boston accent were people around here just don't pronounce the letter "R" when they talk. Sometimes it sounds more like the letter "A" being dragged out when they do say any word that has the letter "R" attached to it. It's just how they do it here, and Dr Harp had that real Bostonian accent that I don't think he was aware of.

He told me he was a blues singer, and that he worked all over Cape Cod then followed up by asking me if I would join his band.

I asked him, "What kind of songs do you guys play."

He said, "We're a hard driving Chicago up-tempo blues band, and we play Muddy Waters and Howling Wolf stuff."

Hmm, I was doing okay with everything, and now I had the time to do whatever I felt like doing as far as playing guitar was concerned. I thought about it for a second and said to him, "Yeah sure I'll give it a try, why not."

I knew the guys in his band, with Peter Ryan on bass, and Big "A" on drums, so right away I was comfortable with the idea, and agreed to join his blues band that played every weekend down on Cape Cod somewhere.

The driving back and forth between Boston and Cape Cod on the week-ends would be a bit of a haul for me, but at the time I didn't mind too much. I was looking forward playing in Dr Harp's blues band. I thought it would be a little bit of fun for me with the nice ocean scenery, plenty of seafood restaurants, pretty girl's walking around, playing guitar with money in my pocket. What could be better in life than that.

Mike, Big A on drums, Dr Harp, and Peter Ryan.

Dr Harp

After a couple of gigs I began to realize that Dr Harp's musical ability was really not adequate enough to carry itself all the way through within a working band that gigs a lot, if any at all.

That is, his playing harmonica was way off kilter along with the timing of his own particular singing method that he established for himself. He just couldn't get it in sync with what the band's tempo was providing for him. He simply didn't inherent any sort of feel for music.

It was noticeable enough that it more or less got in the way of what we were doing as a band. We could get by okay by over compensating his inability to sing and play harmonica, but it was something he simply did not possess as an entertainer.

There was another lack of his talent that would rear its ugly head, and would prove to be one of the more uneasy and difficult episodes of my career as a back-up musician to any of the singer's that hired me to work for them.

During the summers on Cape Cod, lots of people everywhere go down there to vacation for the week, or just spend a long weekend with their loved one, and are generally subjected to whatever entertainment is closest to their hotel. It's usually the nearest club or bar, and we happened to be playing one of those clubs when Dr Harp spotted a man sitting at the bar relaxing. He was enjoying his time off from his job drinking a cold beer listening to the music and watching people in the club mingling with each other having fun.

It was usually in the middle of a song that Dr Harp would walk out into the audience with his wireless microphone then the band would "Vamp", (keeping the music going, but on a lower softer volume so Dr Harp could to talk to the audience).

Dr Harp walked over to this man, and proceeded to ask him. "Are you having a good time?"

"Oh yeah," the man said into the microphone.

Dr Harp continues, "So where are you from?"

The man answers, "I'm a Mountie police officer from Canada."

"Tell me," says Dr Harp, "is it true what they say about you Mounties?"

The man answered, "No I don't, what."

With an over exaggerated "gay" tonality to his voice, Dr Harp adds a distinctive lisp, and says, "Is it true you Mounties always get you MAN?" Then walks away from the bar waving this now limp wrist in mid-air.

I was waiting for the guy to punch Dr Harp out. I couldn't believe he just said that to an unassuming patron just minding his own business that night. But I'll give him credit, the Mountie kept his composer, turned around, and continued drinking his beer.

In search of another victim, Dr Harp found a couple from Maine also on vacation, went over to their table, and asks them, "Where are you folks from?"

They said, "We're down from Maine."

Dr Harp then turns to the on-lookers in the club, and said, "Did you hear that everybody, we have a couple of MANIACS with us tonight." Unfortunately it was these very people that would be the butt-end of Dr Harp's jokes or any rude remarks he would make towards them.

It wasn't like he was dealing with a heckler from the crowd who had too much to drink. Dr Harp was un-refined along with being crude which he didn't mind showing no matter how badly it reflected on him or the rest of the band. He didn't seem to care if it embarrassed us or not.

This had absolutely nothing to do with why we were there in the first place. All we had to do was provide entertainment for the crowd so they could dance and enjoy themselves. We weren't there to insult them or take advantage of their relaxed nature.

Dr Harp really needed to be schooled, and I wasn't going to be the one to teach him he had to learn that on his own, so I let him roll on without saying a word thinking that he'll have to be the one to figure it out if he's going to be in this business much longer.

Most of what he was doing musically was more abrasive to the ears. I didn't think that comedy was one of his strong suits either, nor standing on stage in a bar full of people or off Cape Cod walking around, with that damn wireless microphone thinking he was funny.

More than once I would get a phone call from Dr Harp telling me the club that we played in last night called to cancel us for tonight. Sometimes we would be booked to play a second night for them, but they simply didn't want us back. We lost a lot of work and money, too. Plus, our reputation was now preceding us all over Cape Cod, and probably up in Maine and Canada as well.

The only time I witnessed Dr Harp not insulting a crowd was this gig he booked us for at a party on the second floor of an old brick warehouse in Fall River. When we pulled up to the back entrance of the building there were eight guys that looked like they belonged to the Hells Angels motorcycle gang, hanging out at the bottom of these stairs. It was like they were waiting for us to show up. At the time I didn't know if we should stop or keep going, but when we got out of the car those rough looking characters came over and grabbed every piece of our music gear. I mean every piece of equipment all of the drums, the bass amp, the guitar amp, the microphone stands, our PA system, both of my guitars, and Peter's bass. Then one of them said with a gruff voice, "Follow us." We didn't say a word as we walked up the wide heavy duty metal gridded stairs that led up to their private club on the second floor.

There must have been a couple of hundred people already inside partying as we began to set up our equipment, getting ready to play for them. It did turn out to be a motorcycle gang, that one was pretty clear. All they wanted from us was to rock the joint so they could continue to drink while they ceremoniously bonded with their other biker "Brethren" as if being together was the only reason to celebrate that night.

I plugged my guitar into my amp, turned it up to a reasonable volume, and started to play as the drummer and bass player helped me kick off our set so the rest of the evening could now be filled with foot stomping beer drinking music, while the bikers continued to raise "Holy Kane" among themselves. Yeah we played nice and loud, and as raunchy as we possibly could. They ate it up, and whatever hard driving, kickass screaming Rock 'n Roll music we played, only fueled any reason they needed to show their friends before the night came to an end that they were having as good a time as any.

I could also see with Dr Harp there was no roaming around, with his wireless mic, on this gig. He didn't want to take a chance of insulting this crowd. They probably would have thrown him out of the second story window and wouldn't have thought twice about it. Personally, I probably would have opened the window for them, and counted to three.

Biker gig – Fall River, Massachusetts.

I was getting tired of driving back and forth to the Cape every weekend for one more aggravating gig with Dr Harp, so after the biker gig I told him that I was leaving the band.

The only good thing I can say about him was that he always made sure we got paid. I never had to chase him down for the money. As important as that sounds, that's the only nice thing I can say about the guy. It's too bad he wasn't more conscientious like that on other things in his life that had to do with music.

He really did want to be an entertainer. I could see that without a doubt, but I don't think he really gave himself a chance.

MERRY GO ROUND

AFTER DR HARP, I WANTED TO cool my heels and get off the road for a while. Once I decided to get off that merry-go-round I felt that I could catch my breath.

I also had to think about my next move if I wanted to stay in music. The few previous years of playing-out had seasoned me for something maybe a little more prolific (if there was anything more that might come out of it), but I was also hoping the next phase of being a guitar player would not be so crazy either.

The little stage in back at the Middle East Café.

I decided to start my own jam session, something that I would be in a little more control of. I found a place called the Middle East Café in Central Square down the street from the Cantab. It was a restaurant that had a secluded club in the back with a small stage that had a sound system and lighting that glowed just enough for a band to be seen performing there.

Me with guitar at my jam.

With some jammers.

    It didn't take long for musicians to show up on Saturday afternoons. I made a lot of phone calls and put the word out that I was starting a jam. I wanted to attract as many jammers as I possibly could. Once I started working the club I noticed there was one guy showing up every week as well.

He was a bohemian looking character with a purple colored French beret on his head and wearing sunglasses inside this already dimly lit club. He wasn't a musician or a singer of any sort.

I didn't notice him at first because I was always busy with the musicians trying to coordinate the constant rotation of jammers to make sure everybody got up to play. It didn't take long before he came up to me and introduced himself. He said his name was Shorty, then said, "Listen man I gots to talk to you's.

I was really too busy for his much needed attention I saw him more as a nuisance than anything else. He was persistent so I'd step out into the narrow hallway to listen to what he wanted to say, as patrons and servers were squeezing between the both of us trying to get by. He told me he was having his 50th birthday bash there at the Middle East Café and he wanted my band to play there that night. To me it was one more request I'd heard a dozen times before so I asked him, "When is this party to take place?"

He said next February. I said, "Next February, that's a whole year from now." I thought he was being a bit premature. This was already early March so to me next February was still a long way off.

Then he said, "I'll pay you guys five hundred dollars." That got my attention fast. That was more than what was ever offered to me to play music anywhere.

Shorty continued to tell me, "...I got Bobby Taylor, the G-Clefs, Peter Wolf from the J. Giles Band coming in to sing, and this belly dancer." He chuckled.

I said, "Alright, but let's talk later," and I decided to leave it at that. "I need to get back to my jam."

Shorty - "One of a Kind".

Shorty convinced me to show up at his apartment, which I did about a week later to pick up a cassette tape with the music we were supposed to play for those different singers that he mentioned earlier. When I entered his apartment I immediately saw posters of Trader Horn and old photos of movie stars like Valentino on the walls and on the ceiling too. Every inch of his apartment was covered with pictures and posters from the past. There were 45s (records) from the 1950s pinned to the walls of his office and more posters. A "Wurlitzer" record player stood in the corner and a pin ball machine against the wall that was lit up for anyone who wanted to have a game.

His apartment was like walking into a small museum of historical artifacts from the 30s, and 40s but in particular a bunch of 50s memorabilia had more of a presence to make you think you were transformed back in time. I think Shorty was stuck in this time warp that he was obviously comfortable with. He told me he traded 45s singles from the 50s with other collectors. It turned out they had their own trade publication that had an international appeal to it. He was in constant check with other Doo-Wop enthusiast buying and selling records from around the world!

When the following February finally arrived we were ready to play for Shorty's "Birthday Bash". The club was completely packed with Shorty's friends and guests as my band provided the music needed while those different singers came up to sing their songs. Even the belly dancer seductively danced for the crowd before the night came to an end. I thought it was a good night for all of us, especially for Shorty.

(G-Clefs) Payme, Ray, Shorty, Chris, and Teddy heading out to the "Birthday Bash".

Ray taking center stage – he really loved to sing.

Payme and Chris sharing the mic with a party guests.

Shorty thanking Chris - "Birthday Bash".

Although I wouldn't see Shorty at the club again, two weeks later I got a phone call from some voice I didn't recognize. "Yo' Mike, this is Chris from the G-Clefs, one of the groups you guys backed up'd at Shorty's party."

"Oh yeah," I said, "how ya doing…?" That phone call I received from Chris was asking me to get involved with yet another different kind of music, and it would eclipse anything that I was ever previously involved with. I also thought these were generally older guys with that Doo-Wop crowd, so how much trouble could they be? Yet, here again, was another band pressuring me to join them.

The First Show

THE G-CLEFS HAD ALREADY BOOKED a show for themselves in anticipation of me saying yes to joining them. When Chris called me I suggested the little stage in the back of the Middle East Café to rehearse. Fortunately since it was always available for me, we were able to have rehearsals with the G-Clefs, as a matter of convenience. It just made sense to use that little club as our rehearsal space. We could squeeze in a quick practice on Sunday afternoons if we needed it. There wasn't much going on that early in the day, and the two owners of the restaurant were good about letting us use the stage. It was a nice deal I had there, and it was perfect for everybody involved.

We rehearsed cover songs from groups like the Moonglows, ("Sincerely"), the Temptations,

("Just my Imagination", and "My Girl") as well as G-Clefs songs like "Ka Ding Dong," "My Darling Darla", and "I Understand". Those were some of their original songs that they had been singing ever since the beginning of their career back in 1956.

Although it seemed they could sing those songs in their sleep, it was still new to us, so Payme directed, and cued us whenever there was a "Bridge", or a "Chorus" that was coming up during the song. It couldn't get any easier than that fairly simple. We just had to keep an eye on him.

It didn't take long to catch up to the repertoire of songs they planned on singing that night, but just like the Moonglows and the Drifters, having one of their own members playing guitar, the G-Clefs mirrored that same scenario it was Payme who played guitar within their own singing group. Although it was deemed necessary that he would play guitar, throughout their entire career, the G-Clefs always needed backup musicians to collaborate with, if for no other reason than to support their live act. My band would be included now as an updated version to what they needed. Although not the first group of musicians to accompany the G-Clefs and their music, later as life would progress, my group of musicians would be their supporting back-up band during the 1990s. I would have Bill on drums, Dick on sax, Ira on keyboards, and eventually Danny on guitar, then I would be switching over to play the bass later on.

We felt pretty good after a few rehearsals with the G-Clefs. We were all set to go and do our very first show with them down on Cape Cod for their comeback scheduled for April 4, 1992 at the VFW hall (Onset Beach), Wareham, Massachusetts. The G-Clefs had rented the hall for the night and sent out mailings and advertising flyers about their return to performing once again after being absent from show business for so long. The word spread fairly quickly that they were coming back out of retirement, and that night would prove how popular they still were among many of the local Doo-Wop fans that existed far and wide.

Although it would be a huge success that night, in the interim I still knew very little about the G-Clefs or how they came about as a singing group. I just thought they were some small time Doo-Wop group that had one of those "One Hit Wonders" that made the charts years ago, and they weren't heard from since.

On the night of the show I pulled into the parking lot with my girlfriend, but I couldn't find a parking space at this out-of-the-way VFW hall nothing, none what-so-ever. The lot was completely full. I couldn't figure out what was going on. Just then some of my band members came running over to me. I stopped the car and rolled down the window to see what was up. They were so excited that each of them tried to outdo one another in telling me about some huge crowd already inside.

"Mike," they said, "the place is packed. There are so many people inside that you can hardly move!"

I said, "What are you guys talking about, they're all here for the G-Clefs?"

"Yeah, I think so," they replied.

I still couldn't figure out what was going on or grasp what they were telling me. I grabbed my guitar and amp from the back of my car, and walked over to the side entrance. When I opened the door, wow they were right. I could hardly get through that crowd, it was really jam packed. It was literally wall to wall people. I was even having a hard time trying to get over to the stage to drop off my gear.

There must have been close to five hundred people inside this medium size function hall. Not that you could fit that many people in there, but it certainly was over crowed. I don't think anybody minded being there so early as long as the bar remained fully stocked. They could continue drinking and entertain themselves while waiting for us to put on our show.

Me and the band starting to warm up the crowd.

The G-Clefs - taking the stage 1992.

When we finally started, my band did a couple of standard up tempo Blues shuffles with little fanfare from the crowd, but when the G-Clefs took to the stage, the place completely erupted. These were true G-Clefs fans as they began yelling, screaming, and clapping their hands before the music started.

Then G-Clefs adjusted themselves taking their place in front of the microphones making their presence known to the crowd before they sang a note which only added to the anticipation, and excitement of them being there. Then Payme counted us in, "1-2-3-4", as we hit the first chords to "Ka Ding Dong", their first hit that climbed to #2 on the billboard charts in 1957.

It was obvious to me the G-Clefs were getting a real home town hero's welcome by what seemed to be a legion of loyal fans. I certainly didn't expect anything like this, that's for sure, only because it was so far from Boston.

I was still trying to wrap my mind around this frenzy from their fan's response because I more or less couldn't believe what I was seeing for the first time that night playing with the G-Clefs. This was not what I expected when I arrived earlier getting ready to go to work for them. It completely caught me off guard.

With most gigs I'd done before joining the G-Clefs you had to build an audience up to that point before the night came to an end. But here, the expectations mixed in with a couple of drinks before show time seemed to have pushed that level of excitement even before the night got started.

The show did go extremely well for what little time we put into preparing for it. I was more pleased with what I thought would to be a one-time gig with the G-Clefs, and felt that we had pulled it off in a big way for them. All of us were completely happy about the way it went down, but personally I was more relieved than anything else. Not only did we do a good job backing them up, but we prevailed as professional musicians, and that counts for everything when a gig comes out of nowhere like this.

Although the G-Clefs were smooth in front of a receptive crowd, I could tell they had done this before. I thought at best it would be a little sketchy going in to do a show with minimal preparation, but the G-Clefs proved how good they really were at singing and performing for an audience that expected to see a good show that night.

After the show we went upstairs to our dressing room, and started a small impromptu and well deserved celebration. It turned into more of a jubilation than anything else. Of course we felt we really had something deserving congratulations as their friends and family joined us in the continued celebration before the night finally came to an end.

Shorty in the middle with, Payme and Ilanga.

Mike and Bill.

Just having done this show made me realize that the G-Clefs were somebody big at one time, even if it was from another place and time with years gone by. I had no idea that this type of music would return, sparking life back into a seemingly extinct music that disappeared years before.

Celebration .

There was definitely something brewing on the horizon you could sense it if nothing else. But, none of us could imagine what was coming our way. It would change everything for me as a professional musician only because up until then I was more use to playing the small bars and clubs that existed throughout the region. I could see that this Doo-Wop/Oldies music had another side to it, and it would be different than anything I would ever again be involved with.

This really had potential, if handled properly and if there was any truth about having luck in this business it would only be a matter of time before it might come our way.

Although it would be another evening of that Doo-Wop music being played in our small corner of the world, it was about to re-emerge on a larger scale than what this night seemed to promise for these loyal Doo-Wop fans who thought about coming out that night for a little fun, seeing their G-Clefs sing again.

It was a long drive back home, but I had something to think about as I made my way through what was left of the night, maybe not realizing that some sort of divine intervention had taken place as it presented itself not only for me, but for the G-Clefs as well.

Shorty's Doo-Wop Show

SHORTY, THE GUY WHOSE 50th birthday bash we played for was now getting into the business of being a concert promoter himself. He could see the potential of where this Oldies music was going as it started to pick up steam and gain traction. He made plans for himself to be part of it.

With his various contacts made over the years, he was able to pull his own show together scheduled for September 13, 1992 at the Pilot House Club, on Northern Avenue, in Boston.

The G-Clefs performing at Shorty's Doo-Wop show – Boston.

Shorty hired the G-Clefs, obviously because he knew them on a personnel level and they sang at his birthday bash. He also hired the Dubs, and the Vocaleers two groups I'd never heard of before.

G-Clefs Boston, Ma – September 1992.

To save himself a little money, Shorty wanted my band to back up the Dubs, and the Vocaleers who were sharing the same "bill" that night with the G-Clefs.

The Dubs reached # 23 on the Billboard Hot 100 charts with "Don't Ask Me to be Lonely" and # 72 with "Could this be Magic" during the year 1957. The Vocaleers also had a hit during the 50s called "Is it a Dream".

With another quick rehearsal with the G-Clefs getting ready for Shorty's show that's when Chris felt compelled to ask me, "Do you guys have a name for your band yet?"

Right off the top of my head I said, "Yeah the Bluebirds", but not really being serious about what I just said to him. We were under a lot of pressure in learning new songs for the other groups coming in that night that having a name for my band was not something I was really thinking about. It just wasn't on the top of my priority list.

"No," Chris said to me, "there's already a group by that name, you'll have to pick another one."

I didn't know what to say, I thought he was kidding me, but once I realized he was serious, I said "Chris, I'll have to get back to you later. I just can't think of another name right now on the spot!"

As I started to go back to what I was doing he interrupted me again, and said, "Why don't you just put an 'S' at the end of Blue, and call yourself's the "Bluesbirds", you know since you guys are a blues band anyways."

"Alright, Chris," I said to him, "we'll do it like that." It made sense to me, and it seemed that it would work for us at the moment, but it would remain the name of my band for the rest of our time with the G-Clefs.

Not that it was important to me to have a name for my band most back-up bands don't have names to begin with. The only one I can think of was maybe "The Fabulous Flames" who are the back-up band for James Brown, and I think that's it. So, again I didn't see the real importance of my band having a name to go under, but for some reason the G-Clefs did.

The Dubs and Vocaleers were good enough to send us tapes of their songs to learn. We started studying like crazy, but it was still a struggle trying to get their stuff down. This was all new to us having to learn another group's songs. Besides, these guys were from New York so we really couldn't hook up with them and have a rehearsal.

When both of those singing groups showed up for the venue that night, we were quickly introduced to each other in the dressing room, then walked right out to the stage with them, and started to play their set supporting them like we had done it a hundred times before, when actually it was the first time we ever worked with them anywhere. That is very tough to do no matter what kind of musician you happen to be. But, we were seeing another side of the music business. It was at such times very nerve racking having to anticipate the uncertainty of anything having to do with that kind of responsibility; making sure we played somebody else's music correctly the way they wanted it done. But, we did it.

After pulling double duty for the Dubs, and Vocaleers, we got back to more familiar territory by backing up the G-Clefs later on that night.

Lombardo's

OUR NEXT SHOW WITH THE G-CLEFS was on January 16, 1993 at a large function hall usually known for holding wedding receptions called Lombardo's in Randolph.

This would be another one of the G-Clefs self-promoted shows, and again they themselves organized this event, as it too, would turn out to be another huge success with many of their loyal fans, friends, and family in attendance that night.

We would also work with the Dubs again, and with somebody I'd never heard of before, Lavern

Baker. She had a successful hit song with "Jim Dandy" which reached #1 on the R&B charts, and #3 on the Pop charts, and with, "I Waited Too Long", #5 on the R&B charts, and #3 on the Pop charts in 1956. Lavern Baker had brought her own band that she normally toured with, so we didn't have to worry too much about working out any kind of set for her.

The G-Clefs – 1993

In the beginning it was interesting to see how the G-Clefs could organize and put their own shows together. They certainly had the know how and were very capable of doing that, and successfully I might add.

The G-Clefs were their own boss on this one, and I think they were more comfortable knowing they had the capability to go it alone, but it doesn't matter. You really have to rely on other people that can "bankroll" any event that needs support. They have "connections" and the expertise that allows you to continue working consistently instead of once in a while. It's just the way that it is.

I don't think the G-Clefs had that kind of money to support the kind of funding needed to continue with the music side of their lives. It really is almost impossible to do it all by yourself.

BILL

THAT SUMMER THE G-CLEFS were back down in Onset beach in Wareham. This was their home away from home, and it was just loaded with friends and family that happen to live there year round. It was an automatic built in crowd every time the G-Clefs showed up to give a concert. The G-Clefs just loved doing these "Picnic in the Park" type shows for a summer afternoon day.

It was not too far from the ocean so that you could catch a summer breeze with plenty of sunshine that made it a pleasant day to be out. This was a huge park area with a large stage for outdoor entertainment along with plenty of picnic tables and open grills for people to cook food for themselves and their family.

The G-Clefs in causal mode.

It was right after this gig that the G-Clefs told me to fire our drummer Bill, and find someone else to replace him. This came directly from Payme himself. He said they felt that Bill didn't have enough of a "back beat" to his playing, and for me to find somebody else to play drums for them. I don't know why or what the heck happened. I didn't question too many things in the beginning with their decisions concerning my band. I knew Bill could be a bit of a wise guy at times, which would end up causing me more problems as time went on with the G-Clefs, but one thing about Bill was he was always loyal, and very conscientious when it came time to play on any gig. Plus he could make every rehearsal, too.

Me and Bill after the gig.

Bill was one of the regular musicians that came to my jam session at the Middle East Café every Saturday and I initially got to know him pretty well. He was always on time, and he got involved with the other musicians. To me I thought he was a good drummer, never over bearing with his style of playing. He seemed to be right in the pocket for what was needed whether we were playing Blues, or rock 'n roll. All of that did not matter to the G-Clefs now. I still had to call Bill a couple of days later and tell him he was fired.

The only thing I could reason was that the G-Clefs knew more than me about what they and their music needed, and the type of musicians they preferred to be involved with for their live shows.

For a replacement, I asked Cecil, another friend of mine to come in and play drums for us. I knew Cecil from jamming with him at the other "Cutting Sessions" around Boston. He had a good personality, and a sense of humor.

We had one more show back down in Onset before the summer finally came to a close and right after we played that gig Ilanga had paid me in cash for the band. I put the money in my pocket and went to search for my other band members so I could pay them.

As I was walking across the short end of the field I could see my guys loading up their cars with their equipment, but I was interrupted when I got jumped by one of the party goers that had been there all afternoon. At first I didn't know what was going on. I thought it was a fan or a friend of mine fooling around, maybe just little bit over excited. I had been through things like that before so I just thought it would be over as quickly as it had started. But whoever it was turned out to be some guy actually trying to mug me. He somehow knew I just got paid and that I had the band's cash on me.

He jumped on my back from behind, but he immediately fell off. I turned around to see what kind of moron was trying to push me to the ground. When I did the guy got back up, but this time he lunged at me trying to bear-hug me hoping this time to take me to the ground.

My saving grace was that this guy had been drinking all afternoon and was too drunk to pull any kind of a robbery attempt. Once he realized it, he simply staggered away.

I couldn't believe that sort of thing would happen at this informal affair with family and friends in plain sight like that, but it did. I learned not to let my guard down again anywhere else.

Boston City Hall Plaza

IT WAS AUGUST 10th, 1994, and I knew this would be my first show where we would play in front an audience this large. There were at least three thousand people there that night waiting for a free concert sponsored by the City of Boston's concert series on their performance stage at City Hall Plaza.

Up to that point I was playing small bars, and clubs or somebody's backyard for their BBQ in the middle of a warm summer day while people drank beer by the swimming pool, relaxing, enjoying the music.

This was more of a concert setting with a pro sound system, a suspended lighting system over the stage, and roadies moving our equipment on and off stage for us.

Sound check at Boston's City Hall Plaza.

Me With Mayor Menino – Boston.

The audience that night was enthusiastic and gave us a warm reception when we took to the stage. It was one of those good gigs you get to do when everything goes your way. A beautiful night the Mayor of Boston introduced us to the crowd, and the G-Clefs singing their hearts out. I think they were trying to prove that they were still around, and very much alive and well.

Ray with Teddy up top and Ilanga to the side.

Show time – Boston 1994

Teddy and Payme.

At our next rehearsal, I suggested to the G-Clefs that whatever you do, don't turn down any gig that might come our way. I thought the more work we had, the tighter, and better we would become as a musical unit all the way around.

Sometime later when they told us we were doing another small-time Bar Mitzvah gig I asked, "How come we're doing a Bar Mitzvah gig?"

Chris turned very quickly to me, raised his voice and said, "Well you said not to turn down any gig!" Yeah he was right. I forgot I actually said that, but I was thinking more on the line of larger shows like that City Hall gig we did a month earlier bigger crowds and better exposure for us, maybe bigger money too. I thought that wouldn't be so hard to take, but I still got taken down a notch by Chris that day.

We continued to pick up smaller gigs, playing birthday parties, both children, and adults, and of course, something every musical band eventually has to do, weddings. Before we finished another gig for a young girl's Bat Mitzvah party being celebrated in Newton, Payme pulled me aside and told me to call Bill and have him come back in to play drums again. It seemed the G-Clefs didn't like Cecil either.

I now had to fire another drummer and a friend from my band. I was glad to hear they wanted Bill back in the band, but Cecil was very good and he came in with a professional attitude which is what I was looking for.

When I called Cecil to tell him he was fired, he was very good about it, "No problem," he said, "man that's just how it is in this business." I really did feel bad about that one.

With Bill back we would have another quick rehearsal at the Middle East Café for another small gig we were booked for, and we were up and off to the races once again. Fortunately for us, Bill picked up right where he left off.

Even though we were still playing more birthday parties, and weddings, I thought as long as we were gigging we would be alright. At that point I wasn't concerned about what types of gigs we had. The fact we had a gig was on acceptable terms with me.

I stopped thinking about larger shows like the one we did back at City Hall Plaza a few months earlier. I had to leave that thought behind. For now it would remain a pleasant but distant memory.

Rita

APRIL 22, 1995 WE WOULD do another adult birthday party for a friend of the G-Clefs named Rita. It was a surprise from her kids, and it would be completely filled with her friends and family at another VFW function hall they rented in Roxbury just outside of Boston.

From the beginning of our involvement as a band with any of the G-Clefs shows we would usually have two quick rehearsals with them a couple of weeks in advance of a show and that would usually be it. It's what I call a "Soft Touch", just a quick go through with them, and anything else that had to do with their songs we'd learn them on the "fly". Again nothing too constricting or serious considering what we were doing; just enough rehearsing to get us through any of their gigs coming up somewhere. Then after the gig was over, I wouldn't hear from the G-Clefs for another month or two.

I always thought we really needed to put in a little more work to improve our show, but we really didn't have the time to be on the more professional side. It was a lack of time to commit to having more rehearsals. We all had day jobs and whatever time off we had was usually spent with family or friends.

We could tell that what we were doing was a bit weak and could be better if we truly worked on the music. I know we had the potential to be a bit more polished than what we were doing. At our next meeting I pointed out that all of us needed to start a better regiment towards getting ready for future shows. I thought that maybe I was coming across as too pushy or too bossy with this suggestion but when I didn't hear anybody object to what I suggested I knew it was "in the bag".

I lobbied for us to start having weekly rehearsals amongst ourselves. The G-Clefs on their own on Saturday, and my band members (the Bluesbirds) would get together every Saturday. Then the two groups would meet on Sunday afternoon for a full band rehearsal.

Once we all agreed to it, it was now a matter of keeping the music a little more solid between us, if nothing else. I didn't want to wait another month or two before we got back together again. It always seemed like we were starting from scratch, and just like that old saying, "out of sight, out of mind".

On the phone networking the group.

Taking and giving directions.

As we started moving in the right direction I also thought we should have been doing the more popular Doo-Wop oldies songs that you always heard on the radio like "Earth Angel"; "Blue Moon" or "Two Silhouettes on the Shade"; those types of cover songs! Songs that people would instantly recognize. I think that would have broadened our appeal a little bit more and kept us on the more marketable side to any of the Doo-Wop oldies shows that were starting to become more abundant, but the G-Clefs wanted to stick with their own repertoire of songs that they wrote and were known for. Not that we completely disregard cover tunes, but it was what they wanted to focus on.

Sometimes if a new song was introduced to us at a rehearsal the G-Clefs definitely wanted to have it ready for our next show, but some of those songs required more thought and time in order to play it to make it work right.

One of those songs was called "Can't Do Sixty No More", by the Du Droppers great, great song. We spent countless hours on it. It's a swing tune that has an off-beat syncopation during the "start and stop" section of the song when it reaches the third influx of a verse. The lead vocal breaks in with the next verse to continue the song forcing it to come in on the back beat.

It was actually pretty sophisticated for a song that was released back in September of 1952. When we finally got it together after pounding away at it for so long, we incorporated it permanently into our set. Both the G-Clefs and my band just loved that song because we really shined every time we played it at our shows.

I think the G-Clefs wanted it because they knew nobody else out there would have it in their repertoire. It would have been too difficult putting the time into it like we did. I'll have to admit the G-Clefs were right on this one.

FALMOUTH

OUR NEXT SHOW WAS MAY 27TH, 1995 at the VFW function hall in Falmouth, on Cape Cod. Believe me when I say that it's a long ride driving from Boston to Falmouth. It's a long ride no matter how you slice it. Even if you lived in the town of Falmouth itself, it would have been a long drive for you just to get to this show we were doing that night.

Falmouth is just one of those places I always hated when I was in the limo business. To me it always seemed like you were driving to the end of the earth just to get there. I've done that ride many times especially during the summer months trying to get somebody from Logan airport in Boston, to Woods Hole in Falmouth just so they could catch the last ferry going over to Martha's Vineyard.

(Un-oh) – Ray's and Teddy's reaction.

Teddy, Ilanga, Chris, and Payme (in background) – Falmouth.

This gig would be a rarity for the G-Clefs because there wasn't much of a turn out at all. Hardly anybody came out for the show. Our friends, family members and even our faithful fans couldn't make the trip except for a few people who drifted in and out that happened to live nearby.

Again the place was pretty much empty except for the locals sitting at the bar watching a game on the TV set suspended above the back corner of the bar. Even the bartender was leaning against the varnished topped bar with his arms crossed watching the game, it was that slow for him too.

The promoter was a personal friend of the G-Clefs, and not very experienced with organizing any kind of show. He just didn't advertise well enough to sell tickets, or coordinate the necessary phone calls and mailings you need to do in order to have a successful show. Yes, granted that's how you learn, but we had come a long way, and I would duly note that this would be the last time we worked for the guy. The least he could have done was to think about having it closer to Boston or something. I think that might have worked out a little better for all of us involved.

To add to the misery, as I was making my way down to the gig my car started to give me trouble on the highway. The radiator overheated, so I pulled off to the side of the road to see if I could find water for the engine. I was in the middle of nowhere with absolutely nothing around in what seemed like a remote, and desolate area. I was too far from any kind of help, but I got lucky. There was a small stream nearby where I was able to get water for that sizzling radiator. After that engine had cooled itself down, I was back on the road, and made it in time for the show. That car I was driving was a real heap, it was old, and totally worn out. It had had enough and was more than ready for the local junkyard.

Michael Feldman

There was one very loyal friend the G-Clefs had, and that was Michael Feldman who had a good sense of humor. Michael had known the G-Clefs from their early days when they were growing up together as young teenagers in Boston. He always came to our gigs or any event that involved the G-Clefs.

After that show, Michael watched me drive off in that beat up old car I was driving and would say to me later, "...you know Mike I'm Jewish, but when I saw you drive off in that car I started saying the Rosary."

Yeah it was definitely on its last leg, and was ready to completely fall apart, or maybe die on me somewhere, but I was hoping it would get me to one more gig. That's all I needed out of it.

A month later that car would break down again on the side of the highway. It finally just died right there, and this time it was during a hard driving rain storm that made it more miserable than it already was. There was nothing more I could do for it. I also knew I could only push my luck so far with it, so I just left it there on the side of the highway, and made that long walk back to my girlfriend's apartment, getting completely soaked from head to toe.

Beverly Wedding

THERE WERE ALL OF THESE LITTLE "nuances" with the G-Clefs and one of them was when Teddy would get "SICK!"

That July in 1995, we had a wedding reception to play for, and it would actually be in a private home in Beverly. Beverly is a beautiful upscale town, just north of Boston, and it's along the coastal shore off the Atlantic Ocean.

This was a beautiful home and everything about it was big, including the dining hall where the reception would be held. That's where we would be playing for their wedding guests later on that afternoon as they would dance and party enjoying a warm summer night in celebration. Earlier everybody in the group showed up on time just to unload their equipment and get it set up for the reception later on, but the only one that was not there yet was Teddy.

We were almost ready to do our sound check when Ray came rushing into the reception hall. We all noticed a look of a panic on his face as he walked up to Payme and said, "I just saw Teddy pull into the driveway and …I, I think he's 'Sick'!"

I thought what's the matter with that? It's pretty hot out there for a summer day, and the heat probably affected him like it would for anybody else. Without flinching Payme turned to the other G-Clefs and said, "Alright, Chris you take Teddy's baritone part on 'I Understand', I'll do his back-up harmony on 'Ka Ding Dong', and Ilanga you take Teddy's part on 'Moonlight'…Ray you can sing Teddy's part on…"

At first I didn't know what Payme was doing and why these sudden changes were being made to their assigned vocal harmonies right before show time. That was the only question running through my mind at that particular moment only because it didn't make a lot of sense to me; not until I saw Teddy walk into the reception hall.

Oh no, he looked drunk, he looked very drunk! He was weaving side to side as he stood at the entrance trying his best to act sober. He was still a little unbalanced, but he was able to make his way to the bandstand. I just keep staring at him in silence as everybody else completely did their best to ignore him. No wonder Payme reacted so quickly when Ray told him that Teddy was "Sick", and I just figured out what "Sick" meant it was their code word for "Drunk".

We had plenty of time before the reception started and we were told we could have the master bedroom upstairs because it was one of the few rooms that had an air-conditioner in the window.

As beautiful as this house was, it did not have central air-conditioning, so all of us disappeared pretty quickly to the upstairs bedroom. We literally needed to cool down, and piece things together and maybe try to relax a little bit and get our thoughts in order. Teddy was in no condition to sing, and the other G-Clefs had to figure out what to do next.

As I was standing in front of the A/C with my other band mates we watched the G-Clefs get into it with Teddy telling him he knew better, and what are you thinking showing up drunk, when all of a sudden the bedroom door opened. It was the bride with one of her bridesmaids. They both came rushing in making a bee-line to her make-up table.

"No," she said as she sat down taking off her veil, "you guys are fine. It's so hot out there I need to re-touch my makeup and my hair. Anyways I have to go back downstairs we're about to start, everybody's waiting for me." Just as fast as she came in, she was gone again, then the G-Clefs turned around and went right back at it scolding Teddy.

Getting a booking for any New Year's Eve job whether it was at a high-end hotel like the Ritz-Carlton, or any up-scale night club anywhere around Boston was out of the question for us. It was not possible for us to think about working that night when most bands were out there playing "Auld Lang Syne" somewhere as revelers would be counting down the clock before it finally struck midnight. It was never going to happen for us. That was the only drawback and as much as we definitely felt left out, it was something we subscribed to as one of the terms in belonging to this group.

It was never explained to us in the beginning but more out of respect for Teddy. He would definitely drink to get drunk, and he had his reason. One of Teddy's daughters was killed on "New Year's Day" while walking back home. An oil heating delivery truck had jumped the curb, and got up onto the sidewalk that she and her friends were walking on. She was killed instantly. So maybe Teddy just drank to forget, I don't know, but I'd have to leave it at that.

SCULLERS

SEPTEMBER 3rd, 1995, WAS A RARE opportunity for us to play at Scullers Jazz Club at the Double Tree Hotel along the Charles River in Boston. This was a nice gig for us, and it came by the way of Steve Marvin a good friend of the G-Clefs.

Ray

Ilanga, Steve, and Chris

Ilanga, Teddy, Chris and Payme

Although the venue is set up mostly for jazz music, Steve who happened to work there on a regular basis with his jazz group asked us to come in to do a show at Scullers.

It's a very classy upscale and sophisticated night club on the third floor. It has dark rich walnut paneled walls with massive oversized windows that look out over the Charles River were you can clearly see Harvard University with the few "Georgian" architected domed steeples that stand out like beautiful sculptures and look even more impressive when they are lit up at night.

It's a great view while you're enjoying a drink listening to some world class music, but before we took to the stage that night, I was summoned to Payme's hotel room. He wanted to ask me a question about something before the show. When I walked in his room there was a distinct presence of a sweet natural aroma that I immediately recognized from the strong scent of marijuana still lingering pretty heavily in his room.

I really don't care what anybody else did within the boundaries of this group, I just looked at it like it wasn't any of my business as long as they were functional (most of the time they were) and they weren't too inebriated (which most of the time they weren't). As long as they did their job once they got on stage, I could care less what they did. It was just something I learned a long time ago to look the other way with the G-Clefs. The only one that didn't smoke was Teddy, I never saw him smoke.

This is one important thing I have to interject here before I go any further, and only because it would repeat itself throughout my relationship with the G-Clefs. It was another part of their being as people, and the one thing they didn't argue about amongst themselves when it came to share a smoke of "reefer". I think it actually bonded them together and would remain as a constant stabilizing factor to their lives.

It didn't get in the way of anything that had to do with their performance, but smoking "weed" would be peppered throughout the time we worked for them. I would see them fight and argue over the littlest things, but when it came time to share that "joint", they were patient and calm with one another as if by some mystical or deep spiritual ritual that passing this peace-pipe stuffed with "reefer" would stop any inner conflict they might have had. It seemed to magically erase any previous hard feelings that they had towards one another.

Again this wasn't anything new to me, I'd seen it a hundred times before with all of the bars and clubs I played in, or hanging out in the back of somebody's van before we went on stage. I noticed it in the beginning of my career when I would get a phone call by some little bar band that needed me to fill in for one night because their regular guitarist was out sick or something. When I got to the club some of the guys asked me if I wanted to get "high" before the gig got started. I never did. I was no angel but I didn't want to temp the devil either.

I have no idea where this behavior had originated from, but seeing it with the different musicians and groups I worked for seemed to be just another part of their lives. It's an accepted part of life to them, and has a much added value to the creative side of an entertainer. If they have this belief that their creative persona demands any kind of drug that will add another dimension to their imagination then whatever works for them will still work regardless what other people think.

The only humorous side that I can shed some light on this subject was when we were at one of Shorty's infamous house parties where somebody passed a small "nibblet" of a joint over to my saxophone player Dick. I said to him, "...there's not much left to it, Dick," and Dick responded, "...well then, I'll just use one lung."

Anyway it happened to be a very good turn-out for us at Scullers. This was a classy crowd, with well-dressed people which was something we were starting to get use to as we now catered towards this kind of formal function and affair; that were becoming a little more abundant for us to work if we wanted it.

These were people that had a little money who hired us to provide entertainment for their private parties whether it was at their large estate, or their country club. We were now starting to enjoy that kind of work from this type of clientele and they reacted no differently than our regular fans that we enjoyed. The private party people happened to be music fans as well, and wanted to be part of what we were doing as they too reminisced about the good ole days.

Jail Time

IT WASN'T MADE CLEAR TO ME, and it's not something to bring up in casual conversation, but thanks to Little Joe Cook, it didn't completely elude me when I went to interview him for my book. It was never a subject of discussion during my time with the G-Clefs, and only did it come to light that summer in 2010 while I was sitting in Little Joe Cook's studio at his home in Framingham, Massachusetts.

Me with Little Joe Cook at his Sunday night jam at the Cantab.

"I had an Aunt," he told me, "who had an apartment over in Harlem in New York City. So when I did a show at the Apollo Theater. I stayed at her apartment, but my band had to stay at the hotel next to the Apollo." The Apollo also owned the hotel, and would often put-up the various artists that where performing there for live shows.

Little Joe continues, "...I went to the hotel to check on my band, but when I walked into their hotel room, there were a couple of adolescent underage teenage girls in the room with them. I said to them, 'What are these young girls doing in your room?' My guys told me that the girls were staying with them. I said, 'You guys can't have those girls stay in your room, they're too young.' When I said that," Joe said, "my guys started to throw a fuss.

"I told them that their mothers would be looking for them, but just then a couple of the G-Clefs came into the room and said that those girls can stay with them in their hotel room upstairs. Sho' enough," Joe said, "their mothers came looking for their daughters, and they brought the police with them too."

When they found their daughters in the G-Clefs hotel room a possessive argument broke out between the G-Clefs and the cops, then a full scale fight erupted with punches thrown, and some of the G-Clefs started beating up the cops. It got rough and the G-Clefs were finally restrained and arrested.

After their trial in New York City the G-Clefs were sent off to jail to spend a little hard time locked up thinking about their misfortune.

Wonderland

SEPTEMBER 23rd, 1995 WE WERE scheduled to play at the Wonderland ballroom, in Revere, just outside Boston.

The G-Clefs at Wonderland Ballroom - Revere

Ray

It was another G-Clef crowd that night, and when we hit the stage, we were ready to play as fans started cheering us on. Again there was very little that could stop us now because we were well seasoned as any musical group could be. We certainly had enough gigs under our belt to have the confidence we needed to pull off another successful show at Revere's Wonderland Ballroom, plus Payme had returned to join us as we hit our stride once again and we picked up right where we left off after his short absence.

There were a lot of expectations from us right after we got a very favorable write-up from the Boston Globe Newspaper earlier that week. The article went on to explain that the G-Clefs were coming back to Revere after a long absence from show business.

Not only were we starting to get a lot more attention like that, but we were being sought out by other local newspapers that wanted to fill their paper's human interest section. It was definitely starting to help with our personal appearances, and we noticed a difference with the attenders because everybody wanted to be part of what we were doing now.

Payme had a recurring problem and it would bother him his entire life. He had a bad back from the years of helping move their keyboard player's B-3 Hammond organ along with a Leslie speaker cabinet up and down flights of stairs during the G-Clefs' tour in England during the 1970s. The clubs there are very tight quarters, so there wasn't a lot of room to maneuver that heavy equipment. Everybody had to pitch in so they could get that stuff in and out of the constricted hallways and entrances to most of the clubs where they played. Those B-3 Hammond organs were as big, and just as heavy as a small car, and Payme did some damage to his back that would catch up to him later in life as he got older.

Even on these shows, I told him he was not allowed to lift his amp out of his car for fear that it would put pressure on his already bad back. Usually I would be the one to voluntarily get it for him, and set it up on stage. He still had his original Fender "Super Twin" amplifier. It's a great sounding amp, but weighed a ton. When lifting that amp out of his car, carrying it into the club, and then lifting it up on stage for him, I thought I was going to pull my back out.

A week later I made arrangements with Payme's wife Georgette, for the both of us to go to one of the music stores in Boston to trade that super heavy Fender Twin amp for something that would be similar, but half the weight. The technology today, like with everything, has caught up with guitar amplifiers too. They have the same output, and power, but not the same physical weight to them. We were able to trade that "twin" in for a Fender "Performer 1000". Practically the same amp, but much lighter to carry around.

During our show that night, Ray began to banter with the audience as he started to introduce the different members of our group. It's something that every front man has to do if he is the lead singer. It's just another one of those un-written rules with those singing groups out there that are working.

When Ray got around to making the introductions he would introduce my band members; first starting with our sax player Dick Lourie, but it would not go well. As Ray looked down onto the crowded dance floor below, he saw people standing shoulder to shoulder, and said, "… and this is our saxophone player with the band, we call him (slight pause) …the Dick..!"

There was a hesitant applause from the crowd, then followed by dead silence as they now focused their eyes on Dick who was standing alone to the side of the stage clutching his saxophone as it rested against his body in silence.

Dick with Chris - Wonderland

Man, that's all that came out of Ray's mouth, what the hell! Did he completely lose his train of thought? My other band members turned and looked at each other waiting for Ray to complete the rest of Dick's name. Was he going to finish, or was that it?

Yup, that was it, Ray forgot Dick's last name. He completely forgot it in the middle of introducing him to that crowd. I thought oh man, how can you do that, Dick is the one musician that sticks out from any one of the guys in my band.

I just think Ray got caught up in the excitement of the crowd that night, and just wasn't thinking when it came to making the introductions, but still, that's all that came out of Ray's mouth. "We call him, the Dick." The very next day, I received a phone call from Dick, "Mike," he said, "I've never been so embarrassed in my life!"

At our next rehearsal I suggested to Ilanga, that maybe we should write down everybody's name on a piece of paper or something for Ray to read off of if he gets stuck with the introductions again. Ilanga said that Ray does not know how to read or write; he never learned. I was stunned when he told me that, but I believed him. As small as it was, it was just another problem that we would figure out between the two of us. From then on it would be Ilanga's job to do the introductions to an audience.

I'm glad too, because we would have a lot more shows in the future, and they would be bigger as we started to get a little more notoriety. We just couldn't take any more chances with Ray fumbling as he searched for anything that might pop into his head before his mind goes completely blank again during introductions of the different band members to yet another audience somewhere.

Most of the audience that night was fans that had already seen us before, but there were a lot more people there that night who hadn't seen our show. And that included the headlining act, a duo singing group named "Don and Dewey." Those two guys also had hits in the 50s with their famous 1950s ballad, "I'm Leaving it all Up to You", and "Justine". Their problem was, they were scheduled to follow us on stage that night.

I could see when they finally took to the stage that both of them were shaken by what they had witnessed with our show earlier that evening. They realized how good we were, and how well we went over with the audience, and it was going to be impossible for them to get that crowd back.

At the end of that show, Payme remarked "I always feel sorry for anybody who has to follow us on stage." We were, just as they say in show business, "a hard act to follow". We were that good, and we always ended up being the best on any one of those kinds of engagements, particularly if we were billed with other singing groups.

It was that "take no prisoner" attitude we had when we hit the stage, and once we started to play we opened it up to full throttle. I learned that very early on with the G-Clefs, you came on strong when you walked out on stage, and it would prove itself over and over again with every show that we did with them. It was going to be difficult for anybody to outdo us, no matter who they were. We gave people their money's worth, and they appreciated it.

I also think we were true rock 'n rollers deep down inside begging to let ourselves out just to give us a chance to show people how good we really were. We wanted to be the best that was out there.

Midway Café

AFTER THREE YEARS, I NO LONGER could run my jam at the Middle East Café. It was taking too much of my time now as I started to get busier with the G-Clefs, my job, and my girlfriend. Once I stopped having my jam on Saturdays, the little stage at the Middle East Café was no longer available for us to use for our rehearsals.

We did find another temporary place called the Midway Café which was really a small working blue collar bar over in Jamaica Plain, just outside of Boston. It's a real scruffy place, not very clean, the dance floor is worn, and the windows are dirty. It has a torn up look to it that emulates this real working class character to it where you can get yourself a cheap bottle of beer and dance to the music played there on the week-ends.

I was telling Ron Downs, our bass player at the time that we didn't have a place to rehearse, and if he knew of a place to keep his eyes and ears open. A couple of days later Ron called me and said that the Midway Café was available for us if we want it.

He personally knew the owner from playing gigs there with a couple of R&B/Blues bands he belonged to. It was good timing on Ron's part because we simply ran out of places to hold rehearsals. I appreciated Ron coming through like he did with his one and only contact that allowed us to occupy the Midway stage on Sunday afternoons.

I thought it was great, it wasn't too bad. Besides if it was large enough for any of the rock bands that came and played there on Friday and Saturday nights, then it would be large enough for us to set our equipment up, too. Nothing fancy about the place, but it served its purpose for what we needed.

The Midway Café

After we settled in, the Boston Globe newspaper thought it was a good idea to have an interview with all of the G-Clefs during one of our rehearsals at the Midway. It would be convenient for everybody involved because it was close to their newspaper plant in Boston.

Before the reporter and photographer showed up that day there was another argument between Payme and a couple of the other G-Clefs, and it got ugly. Even the few patrons at the bar put down their pint of beer, stopped watching the football game on TV, and focused their attention towards the stage that we always confiscated on Sunday afternoon.

Payme was at the top of his voice again as he complained loudly in his usual threatening manner that the others were not doing their parts the right way. The worst thing was that I couldn't get him to settle down. He was getting himself all worked up as he continued to vent out his anger.

What set him off were the usual problems the other G-Clefs were having with not singing one of the songs correctly. I will agree with Payme on this only because he was right. The song we were working on was "Spanish Harlem". It was a song we were familiar with by Ben E. King; his first hit away from the Drifters in 1961. That song was written by Jerry Leiber, and it ranked #15 on Billboards charts that same year, but while we were working on the song, instead of waiting for the solo to finish first, Teddy came back in to it too soon. He simply "stepped" on the solo part of the song, and when he did that, it would throw the song, and the band completely off kilter. After about 3 or 4 times of playing the song like that, Payme had enough, and started to chew Teddy out for missing his "cue".

This is also where I can clearly pinpoint where I'd finally had enough of Payme's outbursts. It just wasn't acceptable to me anymore. Previously I would be petrified with the thought that I had to find the courage to say something to him, but I was past that now because I was completely fed up with his temper.

The Midway was a new place for us, and I didn't want to be kicked out of our first, and maybe our last "oasis" that had been made available for us to rehearse in. I turned my back to the rest of my band, closed my eyes for a second, and reached deep down inside to make some sort of rash decision. Either I say something drastic to these guys, or I walk away and not come back! It came that close with me leaving the group all-together, but there was a lot riding on the day, and I didn't want to disappoint the rest of my band. More importantly, the Boston Globe was coming in to do a key interview with the G-Clefs that would give us the necessary exposure for the publicity we always had to have, and now desperately needed for our next show.

I swung myself back around, and moved into the middle of another G-Clefs heated argument that had more or less turned into a screaming match as they were now tearing at each other's throats. "GUYS!" I yelled out, "This is why we are here to work things out…!" I had to raise my voice even louder a second time just to be heard.

I was yelling just as loud as they were when it suddenly came to an abrupt halt. From the corner of my eye I could see the silhouettes of two people standing motionless in the door way, and the G-Clefs noticed them too. It was the reporter, and photographer from the Boston Globe. They seem to hesitate for a moment, but then came over to the edge of the stage, and introduced themselves. They said they wanted to do a short interview for the article they were doing for the newspaper, and also they wanted to take some photos of the G-Clefs outside.

The G-Clefs left the stage with the reporter, and walked out the back door that led to a small patio outside. I kept thinking to myself, now how can they go, and do an interview, and be pleasant after such a vicious argument that they just had with one another.

More importantly how do you smile and pose for the photographer as he points his camera to take a couple of shots of the G-Clefs who are now smiling as if nothing is wrong, but they did. It just blew my mind watching them adjust their behavior that quickly. It was smooth, maybe the smoothest I'd ever seen. The G-Clefs were very friendly towards each other, laughing and joking as the reporter pulled out his note pad to ask questions he had for them and began jotting down any of their friendly remarks towards one another.

It was a complete, and an unexplainable turn around for me to describe, other than a real Dr. Jekyll, and Mr. Hyde personality trait they seem to share equally amongst themselves that day. Probably one of the strangest things I've ever seen them do as I continued working for them.

"Steppin Out"

"STEPPIN OUT" IS A FUNCTION HELD every year in Boston. This is a fairly prominent affair along with being a formal event that takes place at Boston's very large Convention Hall called the World Trade Center here in Massachusetts.

We were getting ready to play that "Stepping Out" show on October 28th, 1995, but I was told that Payme would be out for this gig because of his bad back, and that I would have to handle all the guitar parts myself.

I told the other G-Clefs it shouldn't be a problem. "Don't worry," I said, "I can handle it."

Then Chris added his personal thoughts, "With Payme out," he said, "one monkey don't stop the show."

Wow I thought, no brotherly love here today. I think they were kind of glad that Payme would be out, but still when one of the G-Clefs were out, would always mean that we would have to step it up with our game just to make up for their absences.

This particular year the "Stepping Out" affair wanted to recreate a particular theme using a "Mock" version of the night clubs that existed throughout Boston's thriving club scene during the 50s, and 60s. They created a more simplistic venue of these night clubs that would take place inside of Boston's "World Trade Center".

They decided to keep it in conjunction with the identity of these different night clubs using their original names that were once recognized during Boston's live entertainment industry when clubs like these were popular all across the country for people to enjoy music, and have a place to dance on a Saturday night somewhere within their own metropolitan city.

Miss Massachusetts with Teddy.

Being the formal that it is, people had dressed in proper attire, again women in beautiful dresses, and the gentlemen in fine stylish suits. It also included local celebrities like Miss Massachusetts who would walk around mingling with the crowd where people could have their picture taken with her, or get an autograph.

With each one of those "mock" night clubs, the organizers had invited different musical groups to play and perform live music from that time period. Their guests could simply stroll from one open "club" venue to another "club" setting, sit with a drink, and enjoy the music with what those clubs provided for entertainment whether it was jazz, or early rock 'n roll.

The club we were asked to play for was called the "Top Hat Club". Once again, the large room would be packed with G-Clefs fans, but again Payme's back was bothering him so badly prior to this show that he made a conscientious decision to stay home, and sit this one out. I know it had to be bothering him because he wouldn't have missed playing on a show for any reason, even if his back was bothering him.

Although he worked us pretty hard at rehearsals, and his temper would get in the way at times, it was pretty clear the other G-Clefs were glad that he would not be there for this particular show. I now had to step up to the plate, and fill his shoes with his absence.

At the Top Hat Club with four G-Clefs.

...they could be animated too.

Me taking charge without Payme.

Even with the remaining four G-Clefs singing that night, the performance went extremely well. The crowd was responsive, and of course with some of our fan's coming out to support us only added to our reputation as this authentic Rock 'n Roll act that always guaranteed a good show for anybody interested with what we had to offer for live entertainment.

We were always a good draw to any show that we were part of, and this night would prove to be no different. We also got lucky which happens sometimes. We were able to squeeze another gig out of it from our performance that night. There was a discrete gentleman that came back to our dressing room, and introduced himself.

"Hi," he said, "I'm having a Halloween party this Saturday night at my restaurant, and bar over at Marina Bay (near Boston's waterfront), can you guys come down, and play for us?"

"Yes, of course," we said, none of us had any plans for that night, so it was convenient for both him and us to accept his polite offer, and go play for his party.

After these two back to back shows I was completely spent, but my job was not completely done. I had to fire one more friend of mine from the band, our bass player, Ron Downs.

Chris, Bill on Drums and Ron Downs on bass.

Ron was one of the most soulful Bass players that I ever knew, and got to work with. I thought he was a great addition for the G-Clefs sound, but Ron just couldn't make any of the rehearsals. We were picking up more gigs and it didn't matter if it was with or without somebody that's supposed to be there for all of us. It's an added responsibility and another aspect of the harsh reality about being in a band like this one. A lot of it fell on my shoulders and for whatever reason it had to stay together for the sake of us being together as a whole.

With Ron out of the group we no longer had the Midway Café that was available for us, and I'm sure they were glad to see us gone too. We were probably an interruption to their weekly routine on Sundays, but fortunately we lucked out again when my saxophone player Dick said he might get us a space at U/Mass Boston, but it will have to be in one of the auditoriums. I told him I didn't care if it was in the janitor's closet, just do what you can, we need a place for rehearsals!

Dick worked at the University of Massachusetts, Boston campus when he said that he could reserve the stage at the school's main performance theater for our rehearsals if we needed it. That theater was a lot more spacious, and was more than enough room than what we needed. This was a 600 seat theater, with a big stage for any production that might need the room for large background props or a multitude of performers involved with a production of any kind there. You could have had a full Broadway play or some ballet dance troupe performing one of their shows on that stage.

This was going to be more than enough room for what we needed, with plenty of space to set up our equipment for our amps, drums, and my portable PA system, but more importantly, there was enough room for the G-Clefs to work out their dance routines, and any other choreography they had in mind.

This new rehearsal place was more abundant than what we needed, and it made all of us feel better about being in the group in general. It couldn't have come at a more convenient time for us lucky break really.

As we spent more time with our rehearsals, not everything we did was play music; there's a lot of discussion on the direction of a song we might be working on, especially if it was a new song the G-Clefs brought to rehearsals.

Fortunately we always took breaks in between just to give our heads a rest, smoke a cigarette, and relax a little before we got back to grinding the "axe" again. It was during moments like this that I got to know the G-Clefs on what I call their previous journey where it seemed that they worked with everybody in the music business. I was infatuated listening to their endless exploits.

They would talk about their days on the road during the 50s, and early 60s, and the people they watched from the side of the stage at the Apollo theater like Jackie Wilson, or playing a game of cards with Buddy Holly because they shared the same dressing room with him.

The one story that sticks out the most is the one gig they did with Jerry Lee Lewis somewhere. The promoter for that show rented a beautiful white grand piano for Jerry Lee Lewis, but halfway through his set, he pushed the piano off the front of the stage, and the piano shattered into a thousand pieces when it hit the ground below.

That story seemed a bit far-fetched for me to believe, but I know it to be true if the G-Clefs said so, but when they started to talk about somebody named Anna May, a friend they made while touring through the south, I said "Who's Anna May?"

"Oh, that's Tina Turner." Ilanga said, "We knew her as Anna May, that's her real name you know?"

"Oh I didn't know that," I said.

They also reminisce about being on Dick Clark's, American Bandstand Show in Philadelphia during the 1950s, so I suggested to them, "Why don't you write to him? He still might remember you guys."

"Oh," they said, "I don't think he would remember us."

But I said, "You don't know, he just might." Ilanga did write a letter and received a formal response from Dick Clark's office, a very nice gesture on his part coming back to the G-Clefs in a positive light.

It became clear that not only were they a Doo-Wop group, but the G-Clefs stood side by side with many other famous singers, and entertainers that would make it into the history books of rock 'n roll.

To Bass, or Not to Bass, that is the Question

MY MUSICIANS WERE THE LEAST of my problems, and as far as learning the songs that we needed to learn. They studied and respectively knew how to play their instruments with a real keen sense of musicianship. A skill they processed before joining my band, but it also meant they had to keep up to the demands put on them from both the G-Clefs and me.

I considered that I was lucky just to have these guys in my band, but bass players I found out were not a "dime a dozen" in any part of the music world, and this position I would have the most trouble keeping filled as I worked to keep my band prepared and ready for another gig somewhere with the G-Clefs.

To be our bass player turned out to be nothing more than a rotating door. I was plagued by constant problems trying to keep this position filled. I made a lot of phone calls, and asked friends of mine who would come in and join the band to play bass for us, but for some reason they couldn't stick it out. I also found out that there were a lot of prima donnas out there, and once they joined I heard nothing but every excuse in the world. In the beginning they loved it, but when they realized the work involved, they'd quit.

Bass players are very tough to come by for various reasons, but fortunately I did learn to play the instrument when I ran my jam session back at the Middle East Café. It was how I kept the jam going especially when there were no bass players in the club that day. Unbeknownst to me, it would be the one thing that paid off for me in the near future; having that kind of working knowledge.

I always let it be known that the bass guitar job was for anybody who wanted it. I wasn't prejudiced what-so-ever towards anyone, but experiencing the never ending problems with keeping any bass player in my band would lead up to one of the most daring, and near disasters I had to deal with and avoid, with our Bass player at the time, Ken Larsen.

Ken Larsen

Ken had called me on Sunday morning, just a couple of hours before a rehearsal with the G-Clefs to tell me he couldn't make it; that his car or something had broken down the week before, and he was without transportation. I knew it was just a sorry excuse on his part so he wouldn't have to leave his house.

Ken was a great bass player, but he was the type of guy who didn't think it was really necessary to rehearse with any musical group, even with us. He could definitely cut it on the gigs no problem, but I still went crazy over the phone with him because he called me at the last minute like that.

I told him I just couldn't "start calling everybody to cancel the rehearsal just because you can't make it. It's too late for that now, Ken. What's the matter with you? Everybody else is on their way to our practice space." Not everybody in those days had cell phones so that you could reach them with a last minute cancellation like that.

I told Ken, "I'll pick you up, so be ready when I get there, and I'm not taking 'no' for an answer. You understand that?!"

I drove like a maniac to get to his house, and when I got there, I almost threw Ken and his equipment into the back seat of my car. Then I got back onto the highway, and drove back to Boston. I hate being late for anything, and all this did was get me upset now because the both of us were going to be late for rehearsal.

It was now proving to be too tough for me to keep bass players in my band, and it started driving me crazy until one day Ira said, "Mike you're a good bass player, why don't you switch over, and be our bass player?"

I'm back to bass-ic's.

I really never thought about it until Ira said that, but he was right, this was something that was obvious to the both of us, and with this new, and welcomed revelation, it would be the answer to our never ending problem.

When I moved over to bass, Danny Gioioso came in to play guitar for us. Danny was a great guitar player, and the G-Clefs knew him because he worked with Ray who had his own band on the side called Southbound, and Danny was his guitar player.

At first I didn't care for Danny, I thought it was one more person to kept track of, but it turned out he would be the least one to cause me any problems. Plus, he had strong chops, enough experience under his belt, and the right equipment, and he'd pick up Ray for rehearsals.

That old saying "What goes around comes around" can be funny when you see it unfold in front of your eyes the way it did for me a couple of years later after I switched over to bass.

I was leaving one of our biggest gigs yet, when we were the opening act for the Righteous Brothers at the Hatchshell (in Boston). There were so many people pressing up against the police barricades that we actually needed security to escort us to our cars when we left the dressing room after the show.

I saw no one other than Ken Larson on the other side of those police barriers yelling loud enough to get my attention and like a gentleman and more out of respect, I went over to say hello to him. I didn't want to be rude and completely ignore him, but when I got close enough to shake his hand the other fans around Ken started screaming and grabbing at me.

Ken wanted to be there for the success part of it, but not the hard work it took to get there. Ken made it for one of the biggest shows we had up to this point in our career, but I kept thinking it was like pulling teeth to get him to show up at rehearsals.

That would have been him up there instead of me playing bass that day, but as I turned and walked away I could still see Ken standing there waving at me alongside the other fans who just got through treating me like I was some kind of rock star.

Dick

ABBY, DICK'S WIFE, CALLED TO TELL me that Dick, (our saxophone player) was admitted to MGH (Massachusetts General Hospital) to under-go surgery for an abscess that developed in his intestines. Pretty serious I thought when she told me over the phone, and I'm sure it would require a hospital stay for him as well.

A couple of days later I went to visit Dick. When I walked into his room Abby was sitting next to Dick's bed with both of her hands clutching one of Dick's hands. When I saw him lying there I felt bad about his situation, but it looked to me that Abby was more concerned about something else occupying her mind.

I smiled, and said "Hello" to both of them, but before I could say anything else, Abby blurted out loud "Dick's not going to lose this gig with the G-Clefs, is he?!" I was taken aback by her open concern. It was obvious she thought I came there to fire Dick from the band or something else that might resemble anything that could be just as cruel.

I said, "No, no, of course not Abby, that's not why I came here, I just want to make sure Dick is okay, and to see if there's anything I can do for the both of you, or if you need anything. I didn't come here to fire him Abby." Then added "That's Dick's gig, he has it as long as he wants it, that's up to him, not me!"

The both of them continued to stare at me in silence waiting for me to reassure them with what I just said. Of course, I couldn't think of anything else to say, besides I really didn't think I had to.

When I left, it became clear that the stakes had somehow risen or maybe everything was on the verge of boiling over for anyone who belonged in my band now. I don't know how that happened, but I certainly took notice of it standing in Dick's hospital room that day.

Mike with Dick, and Abby at one of Shorty's house parties – Cambridge, Ma.

Maybe you had to produce at a certain level of expectation or you lost your job with the G-Clefs. There was never a reason to look at it that way, but now this "food for thought" occupied my mind as I continued to search for my car in the hospital parking lot.

My band members always came first, and I think they knew that. This somewhat new revelation would make it more difficult for me because I didn't realize that firing a musician was part of my reputation within my own band. Instead of trusting me, my band members were in fear of me, at least one of them was. I always considered myself to be one of them because I was one of them, but to fire somebody as they lay in their hospital bed was never my style, which was what Abby and Dick where thinking when I went to visit them that day at Mass General.

BRUTAL

IT WAS AT OUR CONSTANT steady rehearsals that I witnessed the other side of the G-Clefs and their different personalities. You can't help it when you're around somebody for any period of time; you get to know the other side of them. We all have one including me. They're called "quirks" and it can drive other people crazy.

There was one side to Payme's personality I call being normal if there is such a thing for guitar players. Before we got under way with rehearsals my time was spent setting up my portable sound system for the G-Clefs, or setting up my amp and bass, or taking direction from Ilanga trying to understand some detail he wanted to discuss with me for our next show.

The rest of the guys in my band were already set up with their equipment, and loosening up and jamming; getting ready for our afternoons practice.

Payme

Payme favored this opportunity because he loved jamming with the other musicians before rehearsals got under way. It was clear that this was fun time for him. It was like he was a kid again bonding with the other musicians. I don't know, but all of that would quickly change as we went to work with the other G-Clefs.

Payme had a temper and it could get to the point of being brutal, just damn short on exercising any patience as far as I was concerned. It was more volcanic than anything I'd seen before, and it would absolutely explode as he condemned the other G-Clefs in full view as we witnessed his anger. Sometimes he chastised them for not correctly knowing their parts on the harmony of a song or if they were off key or didn't prepare before they showed up for rehearsal that day.

When rehearsals were interrupted with that "full tilt" verbal abuse, normally Chris, Teddy, Ilanga, and Ray would just stand around with the one microphone they were all sharing that day, maybe shuffling their feet a little bit, and take that rotten beating that Payme could dish out at full volume with noticeable anger in his voice.

It was hard to watch as Payme spurted out anger that could come to the surface so easily for him while the rest of us just stood there and waited until he would calm down. Then we'd pick it back up again and get back to the song that we were working on before that interruption occurred. But, it would set the tone for the rest of the afternoon as we now spent the remainder of the day almost haunted in a very unsettling manner.

I never saw that kind of behavior before coming from another musician. I didn't know if I should try to figure it out or leave it alone. There really was no angle from which to approach it even if I tried. It was obvious that Payme definitely did his homework before any rehearsal so when he showed up he was ready to get some work done. He didn't like too much hesitation, and didn't want anybody (in particular the other G-Clefs) not knowing what they were supposed to be doing with their vocal parts.

Throughout their career Payme was the G-Clefs musical director, as he was for us in the beginning. It was his knowledge that we relied on because he did know those songs pretty much inside and out.

It was rare, and sometimes strange to watch, but once in a while the other G-Clefs would square off with Payme, but Payme wasn't one for backing down, even if one of the others decided to go face to face with him. A lot of times I would step in to break it up, but it still left hard feelings no matter who thought they were the one that won the argument.

One time we were getting close for a much needed break during rehearsal when another senseless argument broke out between Payme and Chris. It just drove me crazy when the two of them would start to get into it. So, I told everybody else to go outside for a break hoping it would put a stop between the both of them who were now "toe to toe" yelling at the top of their lungs trying to out-shout one another.

The rest of the group left through the backstage door to the outside patio for a cigarette, waiting for me to join them. I was too tired to intervene with Payme and Chris, so I simply walked over to the side of the stage and pulled down the "Master" switch to the "Off" position that controls the lights for the entire theater. When I did that it threw the theater into complete darkness. What little light that back door provided for any visible pathway was now blackened as the door slowly closed on itself.

When it did that there was instantaneously dead silence from where Payme and Chris where standing. As I strolled past the both of them, who are now standing motionless, I calmly muttered to both of them, "I'll see you two gentlemen outside with the rest of the group."

When I got home the phone rang and it was Ira. "Mike," he said, "one more TORPEDO and I'm out of the band." Ira had had enough and put me on notice. I knew Ira meant it. He was somebody I could not replace very easily. Not only was he my keyboard player, but he was my right hand man as well. That was a phone call anybody would have dreaded, but that's how serious it was for me now to keep my band together.

I still considered Ira's statement to be the best definition that anybody could have given to express the behavioral problems that were stacking up and so many misgivings about being a part of this group. It's a wonder that any of us were still holding on as a cohesive unit trying to keep it together.

Although these fights were unpredictable and sporadic at times, it still proved to be very much the make-up from the "One" G-Clef that expressed himself a little more aggressively than the others, and I came to resent his temper altogether.

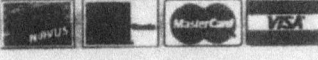

Looking a Gift Horse in the Mouth

AFTER ANOTHER GIG BACK at the Wonderland Ballroom in Revere, I was standing in our dressing room waiting for the crowd to thin out so I could get to my car. Just then one of the G-Clefs came in with a well-dressed man and said, "Oh Mike, this is Rik Tinory."

"Hi, how are you?" I said to him as I reached out to shake his hand.

Both Rik and the G-Clefs went way back when the both of them worked and recorded at Ace Recording Studios in downtown Boston during the late 50s, and they still remained friends over the years.

As I continued to play different shows with the G-Clefs, I noticed that Rik was showing up a little more frequently, and then he'd hang out with us after the show. At first I just thought he was behaving like another fan of ours who wanted to be included as one of our faithful followers.

Rik was a successful businessman building his reputation on his own hard earned merits as a producer, which enabled him to know just about everybody in the music business. Believe me it doesn't hurt to have somebody like him included into your realm of friends.

Rik made a lot of connections over time and thought he could do something in collaboration with the G-Clefs as far as helping them with a little more than where they were at the moment, seemingly content doing their live shows confined to the city limits of Boston.

Rik still had a thriving and very successful recording studio located in his home town of Cohasset. He went on to record Aerosmith's "Pump" album and, Susan Tedeschi's first album "Just Won't Burn". Susan would also have a successful career and would later marry Derek Trucks from the Allman Brothers.

I remember the night when I first met Rik, and hearing him say to the G-Clefs, "... let's do something together." That rings so clearly in my memory because at first I didn't know what he had in mind, but whatever it was it had to be better than where we were as an oldies group looking for a much needed break.

It was clear to all of us he liked what he saw and probably what he heard at our shows. He thought he could do something in revitalizing this music that we were very much a part of and Rik could see the potential it had and what it could generate as its popularity was returning to the forefront again.

We always needed somebody with any kind of connection out there to help energize our struggling career even if it's some fresh idea to get us back into the business of making music. I believed that Rik was the one person who could help get us to that next step.

It took a while, but when the G-Clefs finally agreed to meet with Rik down at his studio to discuss future plans, I really didn't think anything would come out of it, but all in all it wouldn't hurt to see what he had in mind.

A few days later I asked Ilanga how did your meeting go with Rik. "Oh you don't even want to know," he quickly said to me, "Payme went on his trip," which was the code word for his "temper". Ilanga didn't have to give me any more details by now I could fill in the blanks all by myself.

It turned out when they were at Rik's studio, Payme started getting upset and then argued with everybody over something he totally disagreed with. I'm sure he got loud about it in front of Rik and turned on the rest of the G-Clefs before storming out in the middle of discussions.

I found out later, Rik being the record producer that he was, wanted the G-Clefs to record a couple of songs in his studio for an idea he thought might work-out for us. He still had plenty of connections in New York City, and wanted to send the G-Clefs project to some of those contacts.

It might have cost us a few dollars with the recording costs, but it would have also helped us out in the long run, and whatever it was couldn't possibly hurt us none, in my opinion. Nothing gained nothing lost was my attitude. Rik was trying to help us get past where we were as a rock 'n roll group with those contacts he had, and that we desperately needed in order to move forward.

"Would you guys be interested?" That's all Rik Tinary asked of the G-Clefs. It doesn't get any more straight forward than that, and I thought he was being completely fair about it too. I'm sure Rik was also looking out for his best interests but regardless, you don't get many offers in this business without somebody like Rik. This would be the first time I would see the G-Clefs as a whole, look a gift horse in the mouth, and walk away from it.

Rolls Royce Club

THAT SAME YEAR WE WERE BOOKED into a fairly large nightclub near Mattapan Square, (another part of Boston) called the Rolls Royce Club. Our dressing room was just what the G-Clefs had talked about in their earlier days when they traveled the country performing as entertainers for the different nightclubs they sang in, but when they got to the club there wasn't a dressing room anywhere near the place. The basement was the closest thing they had if they wanted to change into their suits.

It would be a repeat experience for the G-Clefs, but now this time with my band in tow. Once we got to the club that night, we were led down this narrow wooden staircase to the cellar to change into our suits.

Like I said, the G-Clefs had already been through that sort of uncompromising accommodation earlier in their career, and I noticed that it didn't seem to bother them as much as it did me. I didn't care standing next to cases of empties and kegs of beer that made the place smell like an open brewery as we stood in place trying to step into our suit pants because there was no place to sit down. It was tight quarters for ten grown men trying to maneuver around without bumping into one another. The only light came from a single light bulb screwed into an open socket that dangled from the ceiling. You had to bend down as you walked around too so you didn't bump your head on the exposed wooden beam that supported the dance floor above us.

With the poor ventilation it was becoming harder to breath as this feeling of claustrophobia started to make it feel more constricting than it really was. I couldn't wait for show time to get to the circulating air above us.

There was a lot of compromising when it came time for any of the basic creature comforts in this business. Sometimes it wasn't much of anything at all, but again, a gig is a gig, and no matter what or where you end up being asked to play you just do the best you can with what's available to work with.

Working the Rolls Royce Club – Boston 1997.

Working the Rolls Royce Club - Boston, October 1997.

Mr. Bob Walker

WITH MY DAY JOB, I HAD JUST dropped off a client in Scituate, (a town along the Massachusetts coast) when I got a call from Ilanga. There was a level of excitement in his voice telling me about some newspaper article that interviewed a local businessman named Bob Walker.

Bob Walker

As Ilanga continued he briefly told me that Bob Walker had been the G-Clefs booking agent during the early 1960s. I thought that was interesting to hear, but as Ilanga continued, "Mike," he said, "he's the one that booked us on the college circuit when we first started out as a singing group. We totally lost touch with him over the years." Then Ilanga added, "I'm so glad he's still around, he'll help us out big-time. He'll put us back out there he has all the connections that we need!"

As I said good-bye to Ilanga I thought to myself "wow, what a stroke of luck this is. Maybe this is the light we've been looking for at the end of this long dark tunnel we found ourselves in; looking for a much needed break." Of course I still didn't know who this guy Ilanga was talking about, and neither one of the G-Clefs ever mentioned his name until now. More importantly the mood around me had changed and it just wasn't me that picked up on it. The G-Clefs seemed to have a real assurance about themselves with a renewed confidence, and whatever it was had come to the surface in full view for us to witness. We all couldn't help but be drawn to this bright light of hope like moths to a flame, as the G-Clefs were trying to impress upon us how important this Bob Walker guy was.

They continued to tell us almost in unison that they just found a very "REALIABLE" friend who was going to change everything for us, and to get ready to start playing professionally. I thought we were already doing that, but I think they meant on a larger scale.

It was that very impression that led me to believe that Mr. Walker was to be taken seriously, and that he was going to set us up doing shows first locally then around the country. I guess he could backup what he was telling the G-Clefs earlier because he had those kinds of connections and a resume that had enough clout attached to it that he could get things done for any one of the clients that he thought about representing.

It was certainly a good feeling that somebody was now going to take care of things for us in terms of managing our career. This new found connection with Mr. Walker made us feel like we had a half chance to finally move forward in the right direction.

Mr. Walker had taken on the G-Clefs in the early 60s as their agent, and booked them throughout the college circuit with steady gigs around the entire country. There were a lot of groups like the G-Clefs in those days that went out and performed and played live shows on college campuses and any "Frat houses" they could play for, along with a small amount of club work mixed in between their travels, as they crisscrossed the country.

Bob Walker was from the Bronx. He attended City College in Manhattan during the mid-1950s. He went to class at night and worked a job during the day. After graduating from City College in 1959, Bob Walker who had a degree in communications, left New York and came to Boston with his wife to start working for his Uncles lecture business, Harry Walker Inc. It brought speakers to small groups. After working there for five years, Bob Walker opened his own business APB, (American Program Bureau). It was the early 60s and one of his first clients was a civil rights activist Dick Gregory.

Other illustrious clients he brought to the college circuit were Julian Bond, Ralph Nader, Abbie Hoffman, Martin Luther King Jr., Pearl S. Buck and Gloria Steinem all booked lectures through APB. After the Watergate scandal APB would book the investigative reporters Bob Woodward and Carl Bernstein and former attorney general John Mitchell and Howard Hunt. Also, Mikhail Gorbachev, Larry King, Rick Pitino, Johnnie Cochran and George Bush, were all clients of APB.

By 1979 Bob Walker had built the largest agency in the world. He soon became president of operations at Sullivan Stadium, now Gillette Stadium where the New England Patriot football team plays. He would bring in the Grateful Dead, Madonna, U-2, and David Bowie for performances there. A very impressive resume, so how could we possibly go wrong with a guy like that on our side?

The G-Clefs agreed to meet with Mr. Walker later that week for dinner to make small preparations and plans necessary for their new found future, but it would fall apart before it even got underway when Teddy arrived late to the restaurant. As he staggered in it was obvious that he was intoxicated, very intoxicated. For whatever reason, he'd been drinking heavily before their meeting with Mr. Walker.

It was clear to everybody at the dinner table that Teddy was out of his mind drunk, and Bob Walker, like everybody else in the restaurant, couldn't help but notice his rude behavior as he made his way to their table.

I'm sure it was there that Mr. Walker thought twice about representing the G-Clefs in any format, whether it was back in the 1960s, or here now in the 1990s. It didn't matter if this music from the G-Clefs was still capable of delivering any kind of selling point to the public, or if we were added to Doo-Wop's growing resurgence that was already taking place around the country. All of that was well on its way, and heading full-force towards being in the mainstream of popular music again. Either we were gonna be part of it, or we weren't. Bob Walker made that decision for us when Teddy walked into the restaurant drunk.

I wasn't aware of what happened so at our next rehearsal my curiosity was getting the better of me so I asked how it went with Bob Walker. Chris said, "Teddy made a fool of himself, he showed up drunk. We had to keep telling him to shut up at the dinner table in front of Bob Walker."

I thought to myself, "What the hell is wrong with these guys?! Can't they control themselves?!" I couldn't even begin to reason in my mind what they were thinking, especially Teddy!

He was the oldest and considered the statesman of the group, but Chris continued to tell me, "… we all knew afterwards that it did not go over well with Bob Walker, it didn't make a good impression on him."

It was obvious that Mr. Walker did not appreciate Teddy's behavior either. This was intended to be a good and what he probably thought a solid investment for him, and now he didn't want any part of us after going through a real confidence killer like that.

The air seemed to be taken right out of our rehearsal room that afternoon when Chris told us what happened. It was puzzling to me as I said nothing. I put my guitar strap over my shoulder and reached down to turn on my amplifier for yet another empty promise as I tried to digest what had transpired a couple of nights before at the restaurant. Even though Mr. Walker had pre-booked us for the Foxwoods Casino down in Connecticut (our backyard) before their meeting, we didn't even make it that far, a shame really.

It was now clear that old habits like Teddy's did not fade away with time. This one would rear its ugly head at the worst possible moment for all of us involved, and now there was no future from the one guy who could have been a real turn around for all of us to go in the right direction and make some real money. That would have been made possible for us.

That was another thing that bothered me to no end. When I first met up with the G-Clefs, I was aware of their financial situation. It was clear they didn't have much in the way of a bank account; that was no big secret. They were still renting apartments, driving older cars or maybe no car at all. I know financially they needed the work we were doing locally just to make their lives worthwhile if not for themselves, certainly for their families. We were all in the same boat financially so having gone through this latest catastrophe was nothing but a real let down for all of us, pure and simple, a real drag to say the least.

What got me the most was that so many times Teddy would openly complain about how Herb Reed from the Platters got a check for eight million dollars when he hired a professional attorney to go after back royalties due to him that he never received from his record company when he was with the Platters.

Ironically both Teddy and Herb lived in the same town of Arlington and they would occasionally bump into one another at the post office, so they knew each other fairly well. I remember one afternoon were I finally had enough of hearing Teddy talk about for the "umpteenth" time how the G-Clefs never received their fair share of royalties from their record company, that I told Teddy to "stop whining about it and call Herb Reed, and get his attorney's phone number and call the guy.

Maybe he can help you get back your royalties you think are due to you guys." I thought it could be as simple as that. It was the last time I ever heard Teddy say another word about it. He never did make that phone call.

Mt. Un-Pleasant

AS USUAL, I WOULD GET A CALL from Ilanga as soon as there was a show booked for us. He said over the phone that we have a couple of gigs, one at the VFW hall down in Onset (Wareham) for July and the other one will be a wedding the following September at Mt. Pleasant Country Club.

While I was writing down the information for these two shows, Ilanga also said that Ray, will not be doing any of those shows with us.

I said, "Oh is he sick or something?"

"No," said Ilanga, "he's on punishment."

I said, "Punishment! What, just for one of the gigs we're on"?

"No," he said, "he's being put on punishment for one year."

"One year!" I exclaimed.

I was completely stunned. I didn't know what to say, and I certainly couldn't think of what Ray did to be put on punishment to begin with. He was the least confrontational of any of the G-Clefs. I thought that this is really going to set us back if Ray is not with the group, but that's the way I always felt when any one of them would be out from a gig for any reason.

Ray had a voice that was perfect for what we were doing. He could sing Doo-Wop, rock 'n roll, or any Motown stuff we played. He had a very strong and powerful vocal ability with the right amount of presence to it that gave it a full sound while adding in a very soulful mix that he was able to project as he sang.

I knew that there was nothing I could do to change Ilanga's mind, or influence what I thought was a bad idea.

Ray Gipson

Ilanga said that he would take responsibility as lead singer for the remainder of the gigs that were scheduled the rest of the year. I'll be honest here, and really to my relief, the first gig we did without Ray I thought Ilanga actually did a very good job singing lead. It seemed to be adequate for what we were doing, so I just let things die down and focused on our next gig. Again I thought we would be alright playing the wedding gig that was coming up that September, but this is where I would see that Ilanga's decision to not have Ray in the group was a bad one that would bite us in the rear.

On this gig, we were given the men's locker room to serve as our dressing room, it wasn't too bad actually. There was plenty of room for all of us to relax and take our time changing into our suits, or putting our socks and shoes on. Another small advantage we had was that it wasn't going to be overflowing with friends, and family. Country clubs like this were a little more restrictive; it's not like anybody we knew personally could go and hang out with us there. They weren't going to allow it

The G-Clefs were very family orientated, and many times our dressing rooms where like you were at some relative's house during the holidays. Our dressing rooms were always jam packed with people. Everywhere you turned there were people making it impossible to move. Most of them we knew, and some of them we didn't. Sometimes they wouldn't leave so we had to get dressed in front of them. We would be standing in our underwear looking for our shoes or trying to put our pants on. It felt odd at first, but we got used to it after a while, it just didn't bother or embarrass us as much as it did in the beginning.

Mt. Pleasant is a fairly well known golf club located in Boylston, not far from the metro city of Worcester, Massachusetts. The reception would be held in the Grand Ballroom for the wedding guests that were invited, and we would provide the entertainment for them to dance and enjoy themselves. That was the game plan, but the gig would hit a major snag before we even made it to the stage that afternoon.

Earlier, everybody was on time for our sound check, except for Teddy. We were still waiting on him as we were changing, but that's when Ilanga came back into our dressing room and said, "I just saw Teddy pull up, and June (his wife) is not with him." Just then Payme stopped what he was doing, but before he could react I could see him thinking with a slight hesitation to his thoughts. Then he said, "Oooh no, when June's not with him, that means he'll be 'SICK'!"

There was that code word again, and this time I knew what it meant.

Payme said, "Somebody has to go tell him he has to stay in his van. He's not going to be in shape to do the show."

Okay, I thought I'd volunteer and tell Teddy to stay in his van. Of course I had no idea what I was walking into. I had somewhat of a good rapport with Teddy always did so I thought he would be reasonable and listen to me.

When I went out to the parking lot Teddy saw me first, stepped out of his van, and started walking toward me. Yup, he was drunk alright, but as he approached me I said, "Teddy, they sent me out here to," ...then, THUD! That was all I said and all I heard.

Teddy delivered a solid right hand punch with a full arm extension right into the middle of my chest. It was like getting hit by a "battering ram", the ones they used during the medieval days when trying to break down the front door of a Castle.

For a moment I couldn't breathe, it knocked the wind right out of me. I was completely bent over trying to get the air back into my lungs, but Teddy walked right by me as if he did nothing wrong. That one really caught me off guard, and boy did it hurt.

As Teddy made his way to the locker room, he made it clear to everyone that he was going to sing with the group regardless of what anybody else thought. Nobody said a word to him. We did our best to ignore him and continued to focus on finishing buttoning the last button on a shirt, or tying one of our shoe laces, just for the fact that none of us would make eye contact with him. It was clear Teddy was in a fighting mood so no one tried to talk him down.

It started to become funny in a strange way as I watched Teddy who was still talking out loud like he was going to give a beating to the first person who spoke up to him. But, being so drunk, he was trying his best to balance himself so he could put his pants on. It took him forever to thread one of his legs into one pant leg, and then steady himself again so he could put the other leg through the other pant leg. It's incredible that he didn't fall over.

We waited until he changed into his suit, then we grabbed him. We found an empty office that was out of the way somewhere and put Teddy in it, then locked the door. We figured he'd pass out there anyways and probably sleep it off. We'll come back for him after the gig is over and take him home.

I now thought this was a tougher situation to be in than anything else we'd been through together. The reality of it was that we were down from five G-Clefs to just three G-Clefs. Ray on punishment, and Teddy who is now "SICK", locked in a back room room sleeping it off.

In one of those rare moments as we were standing around trying to regain our composure, Payme turned to the rest of us, and said, "Alright guys, let's put our hands in, come on." Nobody said a word as Payme extended his right hand into the middle of our small huddle. One by one, we put one hand on top of each other's hand until we had both of our hands on top of each other's.

Then Payme said, "Alright now, 1, 2, 3, break!" We broke from that small circle we formed, and walked out to the stage as if nothing was wrong.

It was one of the few times I ever saw Payme pull us together like that, and I thought it was a brilliant move on his part. It was the only thing we had to reassure ourselves that we still had some sort of solidarity and that everything would be alright. That alone I thought would get us through this already bad situation, but I instinctively knew this was going to be a tough gig for us. I also knew we could work our way through this show just like all of the others where we had different kinds of adversity to overcome, but little did I know that things were about to go from bad to worse.

Once we started to play the dance floor quickly filled up with wedding guests. We seemed to be doing fine until, I don't know how but, Teddy found a way out and escaped from the office we locked him in. From the stage I could see him elbowing his way through that crowded dance floor pushing people aside as he forced his way to the stage where he took his place alongside the other G-Clefs. It was obvious he had not sobered up as he stood in front of the microphone stand grasping the middle section with both hands so he could retain his balance.

As much as Teddy tried to sing with the other G-Clefs, he couldn't do it. Of course he didn't know that, he was too drunk to comprehend anything that he was doing. All he was capable of was to mumble and ramble some of the words together while singing off key.

I could see Teddy trying in vain to blend in and it was obvious to everybody now because he stuck out like a sore thumb. Even the wedding guests noticed his drunken behavior, but they continued to dance as though nothing was wrong. I think they were trying their best not to show embarrassment for him, but it didn't matter if his behavior was overly obnoxious or not because right then and there, Teddy passed out.

His body fell towards that crowded dance floor grazing one gentleman who was embracing his wife and knocking both of them into another couple which started a small chain reaction like they were a bunch of bowling pins being knocked down by a "Black" bowling ball.

Teddy himself slammed onto the parquet floor face first, landing on top of the microphone stand that he was still clutching. There was nothing graceful about it from where I stood as all of us witnessed this small catastrophe unfolding in front of our eyes.

Ilanga had the sense to cover this makeshift disaster, and said, "Oops it looks like we had an accident, but he's alright everybody just keep on dancing we'll take care of it. He's okay don't worry."

I turned to Bill and Ira and motioned for them not to stop playing as Ilanga and Chris grabbed Teddy under his arms to lift him off the microphone stand that was pinned underneath him.

When they stood him up, his nose was bleeding, and now the front of his "White" tuxedo was covered in blood.

We somehow made it through the rest of the afternoon, but this unadulterated behavior in plain view for everybody to witness, certainly did not go unnoticed.

Louise and Donald Production
✺ Presents ✺

"A 1950's Rhythm & Blues Extravaganza"

to be held on Saturday, February 28, 1998
at
The Boys Choir of Harlem Inc.
(Located at 127th & 128th and Madison Avenues)

✺ Featuring ✺
The Willows *"Church Bells May Ring"*
The Deltones *"Take Care"*
The Jesters *"The Wind"*
The G-Clefs *"Cause You're Mine"*
The Harptones *"Sunday Kind of Love"*
The 2 Hearts *"You're Mine"*

with
Todd Baptista as your
Master of Ceremonies

Showtime - 8pm - 11pm (Doors open at 7:30)
Advanced Tickets - $20.00 ✺ Tickets purchased at the door - $25.00
For information, call Louise or Donald at 1 (212) 234-3123

Harlem

AS I WAS STUDYING AND PREPARING for our next show over in Harlem, (New York City) for February 28th, 1998, I got a call from Ilanga saying that there was a slight change in plans.

I said, "Oh really what's up?"

As he began to tell me, he said that, "Payme is on punishment," just like that from out of the blue. Ilanga said that he was not coming with us to do the gig in New York.

I told Ilanga that I didn't think that was a good idea especially on a gig like this one. I said that there's probably going to be people in the entertainment business there that night who could be influential for us, and if we are going to get more gigs from doing this show we might need to bring Payme with us. "I just think its important Ilanga, that's all."

There was dead silence on the other end of the phone. I immediately sensed I over stepped my boundaries, and I could tell Ilanga didn't appreciate it either. I really never heard of these "punishments" being handed out like this, and that included Ray's punishment for our gig back at Mt. Pleasant. This stuff wasn't adding up, and it certainly didn't make a lot of sense either.

The day of the show we left our hotel in New Jersey and drove over to the Boys Choir Theater in Harlem, we had a sound check to do that afternoon before the show. We set up our equipment and waited patiently for our turn while the other singing groups on the same bill did their sound check first.

As he was setting up his drum kit Bill discovered he didn't bring the all-important "ALLEN" key wrench that he needed so he could attach the tom-tom drums and other vital parts for the drums so that he could have a complete kit to work with. Bill had one of those, (half-wrap-around) aluminum tubing multi drum sets that required that special utility tool to put it all together. When Bill looked through his drum bag he realized he left that "ALLEN" key back in Boston, and if he didn't have that stupid "ALLEN" key there was no way he could put his drum kit together.

"Are you kidding me, Bill?" I said.

"No Mike, I left it in my other bag at home, I know I did," he said.

"Well do any of the other drummers have one of those 'ALLEN' keys?" I asked.

"I already asked them, and none of them have one," he said.

"Oh great Bill, that's just great," I said in disgust.

Again those other drummers on the show brought the more simpler kit with them, and were already set up to do their sound check. Need I say more.

Fortunately Bill always had his roadie on gigs with us, so I quickly turned to Paul and said, "Let's go for a walk, we have to find a hardware store, maybe they'll have one of those 'ALLEN' keys that Bill needs for his drums!" Besides I don't want to be the only 'White' guy walking through Harlem in the middle of nowhere when it's already dark out. I already had that sinking feeling of being completely out of my element, and we only had a couple of hours before show time so we had to move fast.

As we started out I was hoping it would be a short walk and that we'd find something relatively soon. I saw nothing but liquor stores, rib joints, and stoop after stoop that led up to the front door of apartment buildings, but not one hardware or convenience store in sight.

I was starting to get concerned as we continued to walk along, but when we started to pass this car tire and repair garage, I noticed this guy squatting down working on a customer's tire. His back was turned away from us, but I approached him hoping he could help us out.

"Excuse me," I said, "do you have an 'ALLEN' key wrench set I can borrow?" When he turned around his jaw dropped opened. The shocked expression on his face said it all, (what are these two crazy white guys doing in Harlem). As he began to straighten up he didn't say a word. He walked over to his tool box inside the garage, and came back with that "ALLEN" key set we were looking for. He continued staring at me as handed me the "ALLEN" wrench not a word from him.

"Wow," I said, "this might work." I told him we'll return it as soon as we were done with it, "thanks again," I said as Paul and I walked away. The man stood silently watching the two of us disappear around the corner.

We lucked out, or shall I say that Bill lucked out it was just what he needed. When he finished putting his drum kit together, Paul and I returned back to the guy's garage. I gave him back his "ALLEN" wrench, then reached in my pocket and handed him a ten dollar bill. "All right," he said smiling at the ten spot, then he looked at me and said, "good man!"

When it was time to do our show we walked out onto the stage for that Harlem crowd as we delved into our already polished and usual set of songs that were instinctive to us.

Harlem Show – 1998

Harlem Show – 1998

Danny Gioioso on guitar in the mist of the G-Clefs.

Ilanga and Teddy, Harlem -NYC

The audience seemed too really like what we were doing, but as we were in the middle of playing "Cause Your Mine" the electricity on stage completely cut out from under us. A master fuse had blown right in the middle of the song, and all of a sudden we were unexpectedly disconnected from the power.

Our amps, Ira's keyboard, the microphones, and even the spot-lights got cut off all except for Bill. The drums are an acoustic instrument to begin with, so he could still be heard throughout the theater the echo from his drums were ricocheting off the walls of this darkened theater we suddenly found ourselves in.

Bill's instincts kicked in as he continued pounding away thinking he could hold it together until we were hooked back up to the electricity. We needed to re-power our silent amps along with the lifeless sound system that needed an ample amount of electricity to bring the G-Clefs microphones back to life.

Bill knew it was going to take a few more minutes for somebody to figure out how to turn the main power switch back on, so he went into an improvisational drum solo that I don't think any of us ever saw him do before. It was probably the only time we witnessed Bill as he knowingly showcased the flair and agility that he possessed as a professional drummer.

The audience started to go crazy began yelling and screaming to encourage Bill to keep playing, while the rest of us stood helplessly silent waiting for our electrical life line to be re-connected. When it did we were able to pick up right where we left off resuming our presence back into Bill's much appreciated rhythmic drum beat; like a giant metronome keeping time until we could jump right back into the song that we started before we were stranded in silence.

After the gig we happily returned to our hotel, but I was told that there was going to be a party for us in one of the large conference rooms near the main lobby. Oh great, that'll be easy to find I thought. I had a little time so I thought I'd take a short nap, but just as I laid my head down, the phone next to my bed started ringing.

"Mike, there's a big fight going on between Payme and Bill, you better get up here."

I said to the woman's voice, "Where's the fight?"

"It's in Payme's room on the 3rd floor," she said.

As I'm running up the stairwell, I'm thinking, "what could they be fighting about?"

By the time I got to Payme's room, whatever happened between them was over, and done with, and Bill was nowhere to be found. I thought it couldn't have been that big of a deal, so I ignored it, and went back downstairs. It was almost time to go to the party and by now I really felt I needed it.

Bill would recall the incident to me on our way back to Boston.

"I was in Payme's room," he said, "and Payme made the comment that the reason why Ira and me can't play this music [I think he meant the G-Clefs music] is because we are 'White'. Needless to say, this infuriated me! If Georgette (Payme's wife) didn't step in between us, they'd would have found Payme somewhere in the swamps of Jersey. I almost punched Payme out, but Georgette stopped me.

"We all went to the 'After' party," Bill continued, "and not a word was spoken between me and Payme."

I was a little shocked that anyone from the G-Clefs would say, much less think, anything like that about any of the guys in my band. I wasn't going to ignore a comment like that from Payme, and I would have to deal with this once we got back to Boston.

A week later we had a meeting at Teddy's and we were told that they (the G-Clefs) had turned down two gigs being offered to them, one in London, England and one in Philadelphia, Pennsylvania. When I asked them why they turned them down they said that they were not allowed to take us with them to do those shows. The promoters only wanted the G-Clefs and would provide another backup band once they got to those two different cities.

The reality of it was that it was just cheaper for the promoter to bring in the G-Clefs by themselves. They didn't want to fly us in and put us up in a hotel and feed us, that's an "added expense".

I told the G-Clefs that they should just go ahead and do those gigs. I said don't worry about us, but they still politely refused both offers from those promoters.

At the end of the meeting Ilanga asked if there any more issues to discuss before we adjourn and I said, "Yes, I have one if you don't mind." I turned to Payme who is sitting between Bill and me. I asked him if he had any problems with any of the guys in my band.

His head dropped down while his eyes remained focused at the floor, "No, I don't," he replied. "Okay," I said, "then I have nothing more to add to this meeting!" I really should have let Payme stay on punishment like Ilanga wanted to do in the first place.

There's an old saying "You can pick your friends, but you can't pick your family". Unfortunately that was this situation we were all in. As much as I liked Payme, he was such a hard-ass sometimes!

Even to this day I never understood him making a remark like the one he made at our hotel in New Jersey referring to anyone of the guys in my band as "not good enough". We really did work hard for the G-Clefs, and I think that was totally uncalled for. Shame on any one of them, really.

The G-Clefs and the Bluesbirds

Rain, Rain, Go Away, Come Back Again Some Other "Mother's Day"

"THIS IS THE WORST GIG WE'VE ever done. We've never been on a show this bad before..." I could still hear Payme talking out loud to himself as I walked past him to make my way to the back entrance so I could unload my equipment from my car.

It was Mother's Day, May, 1998, and we were in South Boston where we were booked on the same bill with Johnny Maestro, and the Brooklyn Bridge; "Sixteen Candles"; Bobby Lewis, "Tossing and Turning"; and Little Joe Cook with his 1957 hit, "Peanuts".

There were strong gale force winds with heavy rain blowing sideways throughout the city of

Boston that week-end, but it felt more like a hurricane pressing down on us rather than some early spring storm making its way through the northeast.

This show was supposed to be a two day event with all of those four singing groups performing on Saturday and the following day, Sunday. The bad weather looked like it was going to stay with us for the entire weekend, and there was absolutely nothing you could do to escape it.

Man it was just brutal it was acting more like a tropical rainstorm coming in from the Caribbean somewhere just to unleash its fuss and fury on us when it finally got here, and anything that didn't get soaked on the first day was going to get wet before the weekend came to an end.

The promoter rented a "large" yellow and white striped circus tent in advance for what he thought would be a huge turnout for one of Boston's premier Doo-Wop shows. As bad as the weather was, he still wanted to press on with his show only because I think he was hoping for the best; that the weather would settle down.

Although that tent could easily hold over a 1,000 people comfortably inside, not one person showed up, that's how bad the weather was affecting people's decisions to venture outdoors.

As the weather continued to make a turn for the worse, everybody everywhere decided to cancel their plans or any reservations they made for Mother's Day. I didn't blame a soul for staying put if I wasn't playing on the gig I wouldn't have been out there either. It was just absolutely miserable to take a chance and dare drive over to South Boston no matter what kind of show had been promised. It wouldn't have been worth it.

As the storm continued to bear down on us, we all took off to find some place dry until we got the official word for some sort of cancellation. It was now a waiting game, and we were all in favor of going home. I thought it was ridiculous to hang around, but the promoter seemed to procrastinate before making a final decision. I think he probably felt he should still get his money's worth if nothing else just to ensure his reputation, never mind the cost and expense of putting on a show that big I'm sure he lost his shirt on this one.

While we were all waiting, my band members found their way to Teddy's van, but I decided to stay inside the performer's "smaller" tent just to keep Bobby Lewis company. He was blind now and I didn't want to leave him by himself.

The "smaller" tent in back was supposed to be a staging area for the entertainers to hang out until it was time for them to go on stage inside the "large" tent, but as I was sitting there with Bobby Lewis, water from the rain started to rush in underneath the tent. I didn't see it, but as soon as I felt it cresting up against the back of my shoes, the tent flap suddenly flung open. It was Danny, our guitar player. He said "Teddy was wondering where you were Mike. He sent me here to get you."

I turned to Bobby and said, "Come on, everybody's in Teddy's van. It'll be warmer there. Besides, we have to rehearse your set if you still have to go on." His backing band deserted him they just didn't want to stick around any longer, so Bobby Lewis had no band if they called him in to do his show. I decided that we could help him out, not that it really mattered at this point, but we were gonna be there for him if he needed us. I thought it was the least we could do.

We pulled out our guitars as Bobby Lewis started giving us instructions on how he wanted his songs to be played. As crowded as it was in Teddy's van, we were able to get the make shift rehearsal together for Bobby.

I sensed he was relieved that we were even capable of playing the way he wanted us to, and sure enough just as we finished, somebody started knocking fairly hard on the side of the van yelling out, "... hey you guys it's time to go on."

"Alright Bobby," I said to him, "here we go." He grabbed hold of my arm as the both of us stepped out of the van and leaned into the wind that was still blowing rain horizontally across the parking lot. My other band members stayed close behind using us as a human shield to protect themselves from the wind as we made our way to the side entrance to that "large" circus tent.

Playing Bass for Bobby Lewis – Boston.

We stepped up onto the stage, plugged in our guitars then Bill counted us in as we now swung into Bobby Lewis' set for the few fans that decided to stick around while we played with one of rock 'n roll's true legends and pioneers.

TRB Enterprises presents
PIONEERS OF RHYTHM & BLUES
In Concert
Saturday, June 13, 1998
Holiday Inn Ballroom, Taunton, MA
(Bay Street Exit off Route 495)

Doors Open at 7:30 PM

Willie Winfield & The Harptones
"Life Is But A Dream"
"Sunday Kind Of Love"

Ruth McFadden
"Darling Listen To The Words Of This Song"

Showtime 8:00 PM

The All-Original Willows
"Church Bells May Ring"
"My Dear Dearest Darling"

The Original G-Clefs
"I Understand"
"Ka-Ding Dong"

with Master of Ceremonies: Todd Baptista

General Admission Tickets: $25.00
Available at: Music Heaven, 105 Washington Street, No. Easton, MA, (508) 238-7603
                Cheapo's, 645 Mass. Avenue, Cambridge, MA, (617) 354-4455
or by mail from: TRB Enterprises, P.O. Box 50962, New Bedford, MA, 02745-0033

CASH BAR / SNACKS AVAILABLE

The Willows

A SMALL TIME LOCAL PROMOTER Todd Baptista called to ask me, "...since the G-Clefs are doing the same show Mike, could your band also back up the Willows? I'll pay you guys extra money."

"Yeah sure," I told Todd, "it shouldn't be a problem."

By now we were getting use to backing up bands that were coming to town if they were on the same "bill" with the G-Clefs, and if they needed a back-up band. We were happy to help them out. It was just one more singing group, but those things are like walking a tight rope without a net sometimes, especially if we weren't totally familiar with their music.

It's really incredible to pull off something stone cold like that with somebody you never met before until the night of the show to walk right up on stage with them and start playing their music in back of them as they started singing for the audience. Then again we would study like crazy in getting ready for them.

Most groups would send us a cassette tape for us to study their music. A lot of time it was a matter of deciphering those tapes because the recordings were from the original 45 records, and they included a lot of pops and scratches on top of the music itself. The songs were not real clear but we managed to sort out what we needed to help us understand their music and be ready once they got here for their show that night.

Todd's show was scheduled for June 13th, 1998 at the Holiday Inn in Taunton. The other group we would be backing up was the Willows. They themselves had a couple of hits during the 1950s with, "Church Bells May Sing", and "Don't Push, Don't Pull" which went to #1 on the charts.

The Willows, just getting in from NYC.

The Willows – Taunton, Ma 1998

I was trying to learn the Bass guitar lines for "Don't Push, Don't Pull"... the lead singer on the record used the word, and what I thought he said was, "Jip-sue".

I wasn't sure if I heard it right, so I wound the tape back a few more times to see if I understood exactly what he was saying. Yeah, it sounds to me like he saying "Jip-sue".

Man I thought to myself what kind of a word is that, I've never heard that one before, and for the life of me I honestly couldn't figure it out. I just kept thinking what a crazy sounding word this "Jip-sue" is.

Alright, as interesting as it is, I'll just ask the lead singer what it means when he gets here. I'm sure he'll be able to explain it to me.

Ilanga, Teddy, and Chris – Taunton, Ma

There was another heavy rainstorm and it was coming down hard all the way from New York state, past the Massachusetts boarder and up into Maine.

It was already a dark night, and the rain was coming down the heaviest I'd seen in a while. It almost made the ride impossible for me over to Taunton. If it was proving to be a tough drive coming in from Boston, I couldn't imagine those other guys driving in from New York.

It would be another full house, completely sold out as we took to the stage when we backed up the Willows doing their set first, then the G-Clefs would follow afterward with their performance. It was a nice balance with both the Willows and the G-Clefs sharing the same bill that night. You could tell that the audience really enjoyed everything about both of those two singing groups.

One of the most memorable compliments that I'll always remember as a musician came at the end of the show when a couple of G-Clef fans approached me, " Mike," they said, "it was like you guys have been playing with the Willows all of your lives. The band sounded that good in back of them."

I said thank you to the both of them, and went to the dressing room where everybody else were congratulating themselves for a job well done. This is where I had my chance to ask Tony Middleton (the lead singer of the Willows), about that "funny" word that I'd never heard before; that "Jip-sue" word.

"Excuse me," I said to him, "you say this word 'Jip-Sue' in your song 'Don't Push, Don't Pull', what does it mean?"

With somewhat of a hesitation he stood in front of me, and said, "You know…" I waited in silence while he gathered his thoughts, then he said "… It's a Jip-Sue!"

Wait a minute I said to myself, but then flatly said out loud. "What!" Now I was a little more puzzled with this short explanation than before.

He started to make a second attempt to explain it to me, but this time all he did was add a little animation by waving one of his hands. "You know…" he paused again, and said, "uh, a Jip-Suuuue!"

"Oh," I said, reacting as if I understood what he meant this time, then I realized that there was no descriptive explanation to that word. I thought it must have been some kind of "lingo" or maybe a "slang" he probably heard growing up as a kid somewhere.

It was evident that he didn't know himself what it meant, and I'm sure he decided to slip it into the song when he recorded it back in the 1950s, so I decided not to pursue it any further with him. I just acted like I knew what he was talking about, and left it at that. I didn't feel like offending the guy any further by asking him a third time.

"Oh yeah," I said "Jip-Sue. Right, I get it, thanks." Then I turned around to count the band's money that was just handed to me.

Although I never did find out the meaning of that word, and probably never will, no big deal, we had a successful show backing up the G-Clefs, and the Willows. I was pleased the way everything went down as well as it did that in itself I would consider enough of an explanation to any word that really doesn't exist.

The Web We Weave….

PAYME TOLD US ON A REHEARSAL break that he worked with the legendary Chuck Berry. Wow, okay, that got my attention.

Payme said that during a newspaper interview he told a reporter, "I worked with Chuck Berry eight or nine times. I used to be flabbergasted at how he would come to a concert without a rehearsal, without his own musicians, get on stage and tell whatever band was behind him 'follow me'. His hands are so strong, he could get away with that. His hands are very strong on guitar, as if dominating when he plays."

I probably had more interaction with Payme because at one point the both of us were the only guitar players in the group, and it was rare for Payme to say anything by way of criticism towards me. For some reason he never yelled at me or gave me a hard time. Only once do I remember him paying me a compliment when he said that I had "big ears", which means I can hear, or pick-up things that nobody else can. Yeah it's a little odd, but I'll take any compliment that happens to come my way whether I hear it or not.

Payme with his "Prized Possession"

As long as he has owned that Red 1967 Gibson ES335 electric guitar, he never put it in the repair shop to have any of the necessary work that periodically has to be done to a guitar; especially anything having to do to the "Fret-Board".

One afternoon during rehearsals, Payme was getting upset with the other G-Clefs while all of them huddled with each other trying to work out their assigned harmonies. It was just Payme with his guitar and the others trying to hone in on their vocal parts with one of the songs we were doing for our next show.

It just wasn't going well because somebody was always off key somewhere. It was difficult to pin point were the problem was, and Payme was getting frustrated and couldn't understand why the others were not on their mark, but again it wasn't their singing. As I stood there watching them struggle, I too could hear something that wasn't right. I said, "Payme, let me see your guitar, please."

When he handed it to me I could see right away that the frets were completely worn down, pretty much nothing left to them really. So when the strings were pressed down, there was very little fret for them to get any kind of friction needed to obtain a clean, clear sound from the guitar. It was time and well over due, and that guitar needed to be put in the shop, but Payme didn't think so. I had to convince him that it did.

No wonder the other G-Clefs couldn't find their harmonies that day that guitar was proving to be impossible to follow. It was completely out of alignment with itself.

I told Payme after the Gregory Hines gig, "I'm taking your guitar with me. I'm bringing it to my guitar repair guy to replace those worn down 'frets'."

Sheepishly Payme agreed, but I could tell he was going to hold off and procrastinate as long he possibly could. But, I was still determined to bring that guitar over to Richard Stanley's shop whether Payme thought it needed work on it or not.

After that show, Payme tried to sneak out of the hotel. He thought I wouldn't see him, but I was looking for him. When I caught him, Payme had his guitar case with him. I quickly grabbed one end of it and right away the both of us started having a tug-of-war with it in the middle of the hotel lobby. I had one end of the guitar case and Payme had the other end as we pulled back and forth, each of us trying to claim ownership to it.

Guests checking in at the front desk stopped to watch us wrestling with his guitar case as the both of us struggled to gain control of it. After I finally persuaded Payme to let me take his prized guitar with me, (he finally surrendered) the very next day I drove over to Richard Stanley and dropped it off.

A week later I received a call from Richard, "Mike" he said, "Payme's guitar is ready but I want to show you something when you get here."

"Yeah okay," I said.

When I got to his shop Richard said, "I want you to see this." He lifted the guitar, and angled it towards me so I could see inside the body of the guitar through the "f-hole." (The f-hole is that kind of funny looking long-gated letter "S" shape you see on those kind of guitars).

As I'm looking, I said, "Yeah I see something, but what is that? It looks like cotton balls, or something!"

Richard said, "Those are spider nests, and there's two of them."

I said, "Spider Nests?!"

"Yeah," he said, "there's nothing in them anymore. They've probably been inside Payme's guitar for years." I couldn't believe it! I've never seen or heard of anything like that before spiders nesting inside of somebody's guitar.

I was able to get Payme's guitar back to him and in time for our next rehearsal. He was completely happy the way it came out. He acted like it was some new toy that somebody gave him for Christmas or something. I never did tell him about the spider's nests.

The Hatch Shell

THE "HATCHSHELL" GIG IS WHERE I thought we accomplished a milestone from where we first started as a group playing small sized parties being invited to play on a show as big as this one would be a move up for us. I really thought we deserved to be given an opportunity like this because we did something right for a change. I also think we were accepted as a viable rock 'n roll group to be taken seriously and that our relentless efforts proved to be the real reason that got us there in the first place.

On August 8th, 1999 we would be the opening act for the Righteous Brothers on the "Esplanade" alongside the Charles River, in Boston.

Oldies radio station "WODS" always sponsored free concerts during the summers. They would bring in well- known acts like the Beach Boys, Ray Charles, or Johnny Rivers, (Secret Agent Man), to perform. Since it was a free concert to the public, it would always guarantee a large crowd.

Big Crowd that Day – Boston 1999

On Stage at the Hatch Shell - Boston

Preparing for our biggest gig yet, we would have the usual rehearsals at our practice space which by now had become our home away from home. Rehearsing for this gig shouldn't be too much out of the ordinary for us, or so I thought. All we had to do was make it through our usual routine, rehearse the same songs that we've been doing for the last five or six years and go have a nice gig for ourselves down at the Hatchshell. It couldn't get any easier than that.

There seemed to be a lot more focus in getting ready for this show, but it would also add a lot more intensity, and as a result our rehearsals would not go all that smoothly. Both Payme and Bill would walk out in the middle of rehearsals; Payme one week, then Bill the following week. It seemed that the both of them needed to get their point across in their own unusual way with whatever dispute they would have with the other G-Clefs.

After a loud verbal argument during rehearsal, Payme walked out grabbing his guitar and amplifier and drove back home. By the time we had our second rehearsal (the following week), Payme had settled down, and came back to work without his attitude attached, but this time our drummer Bill got upset. I guess it was his turn to have some strong opinion between himself and the other

G-Clefs with a song we were working on. He packed up his drums in the middle of rehearsal and drove home leaving us without a drummer for the rest of the day.

I still don't think it justifies those two guys doing what they did, especially when we were getting ready for a show as big as this one. It was all I could do not to lose my temper and completely blow up with both of them; I held my cool. I still couldn't have been any more furious with the both of them, one Bluesbird and one G-Clef!

When we arrived at the show for sound check, security asked everybody involved to remain in their dressing rooms until it was time for us to come out and perform on stage. Usually at shows like this somebody who's in charge of the event would always come around with questions or give some sort of final instructions to the entertainers who are hanging around waiting.

Sure enough, somebody from the stage crew came to our dressing room and said they didn't know where our drummer was, they needed him on stage for something but they couldn't find him. I didn't know what to tell the guy, I didn't know where our drummer was either.

An hour later when Bill finally emerged back at our dressing room I said, "Where've you been? They were looking for you."

Bill replied, "You wouldn't have found me even if you tried. I got into David Ugar's office [the official organizer and big boss man for the Hatch Shell], it was unlocked so I went in."

"What?!" I said, but Bill told me to relax, "...all I did Mike, was sit at his desk, and played with his computer. Then I went downstairs under the stage were the lockers for the Boston Symphony Orchestra musicians are. When I opened one of the lockers I found a Piccolo." He continued to tell me about his wandering adventure like he was proud of what he was doing. Then he said, "...it was funny, when I started to play that thing someone shined a flashlight on me. It was one of the State Police Troopers. He asked me what I was doing down here. I told him I was with the band. He said, 'I don't care who you're with, you don't belong down here, now get out!'"

It was a bit difficult for me to comprehend what Bill just told me, but in a way I was glad they didn't completely force him from the premises. I keep thinking "why here Bill? This is the wrong place to get into trouble, besides what possessed you to think you could even do something like that?" I didn't understand that one at all.

The one time I stepped out of the dressing room to go use the bathroom, I immediately noticed a fairly large marijuana joint lying on the floor by my foot. I'm sure it was somebody's from the G-Clefs that probably dropped it by accident and didn't even realize it until they needed it for later. When I looked up I saw two State Troopers standing in front of me talking to one another, and a couple of Park Rangers standing off to the side of them with their arms crossed like they were keeping vigilant guard for any intruders trying to get by them.

I acted like I didn't see that tightly rolled "dubie". Those security officials didn't notice the cigar sized joint that I almost tripped over, either. I certainly wasn't going to bend down and pick it up, so I left it there. When I got back to the dressing room I told Bill's roadie Paul, that when he gets a chance to "get rid of it".

Again it was a beautiful day with the right amount of sunshine, and no humidity. I could see the Charles River filling up with small pleasure boats getting as close to the shoreline as they possibly could so they could see and hear the show. It didn't matter they were going to hear us; Mike Higgins (our sound man) would make sure they did with a sound system as big as what that show provided.

It did sound fantastic once we started playing in front of those thousands of people, and Mike Higgins was one guy I didn't have to worry about too much. He knew what he had to do whether it was for 200 hundred people at a VFW hall or for 20 thousand people at an outdoor concert as big as this one. He never let us down.

Me and Mike Higgins

Once we got on stage to play, I didn't take notice of the Righteous Brothers themselves who were standing on the side of the stage watching our performance. When we completed our show we went back to our dressing room to sit and wait for security to escort us to our cars.

When the Righteous Brothers finished their show there was a polite knock on our dressing room door. It was the Righteous Brothers themselves, and they wanted to talk to us.

Bobby Hatfield said, "Listen Bill (Henderson) and I were talking, and we caught your set. We both liked what you guys were doing on stage this afternoon, and we both agreed that you're just what we've been looking for. We need an opening act just like what you guys are doing for our shows out in Las Vegas. Would like you to come out and be our opening act and possibly come out on the road with us too?"

Each one of the G-Clefs immediately said, "…yeah we're definitely interested in working with you guys, it sounds like something we would like to do. Then Teddy added, we just need to exchange phone numbers, and we'll get back to the both of you and let you know after we work out the details.

It turned out later, and the sad reality of it was, the G-Clefs never followed up on that offer from the Righteous Brothers, they simply turned them down. When I found out later I couldn't believe it! I was completely stunned. I didn't know what to think anymore.

We finally had a good solid offer with a personnel invitation from the Righteous Brothers themselves, but the G-Clefs didn't follow through with it. I couldn't imagine what was going through their minds.

Even Danny our guitar player called Teddy and said, "Did you call or what."

Teddy told him, "No we turned them down."

Danny was more upset about it than I was. The G-Clefs simply turned down the offer to work with the Righteous Brothers.

It was getting harder and harder to comprehend the decisions they were making as we continued doing shows, but something more shilling would reach my ear's when I heard Teddy's wife June make the remark, "I don't know why they [the Bluesbirds] stick with them."

The G-Clefs
☆Chris ☆Ilanga ☆Payme ☆Ray ☆Ted

Gig: Omni Parker Hotel   Thursday, 13th-December, 2001
"New Boston Fund, Holiday Party!"   Showtime-7:P.M.

1st-Set

Bluesbirds..."Get Ready"
(G-Clefs-Entrance)

1. Ka Ding Dong
2. My Girl
3. I Understand
4. Tic Toc
5. Lean On Me
6. Little Girl Of Mine
7. Canadian Sunset
8. Peace Of Mind
9. No One Loves Me
10. Winter Wonderland
11. Walking Along

2nd-Set

Bluesbirds..."Get Ready"
(G-Clefs-Entrance)

1. Winter Wonderland
2. Sh-Boom
3. Work With Me Annie
4. Midnight Hour
5. Imagination
6. Knock On Wood
7. Ain't To Proud To Beg
8. Moonglow's Medley
9. Ka Ding Dong
10. Lucky Ole Sun
11. Amen

The Next Gig: Saturday, 22nd-December
60th Birthday Party, for "Eve"

At, Heritage Hall--114 Granite Avenue   Milton/Dorchester-Line
Sound-Check: 6:P.M.   Showtime: 9:15 P.M.

Performing Same Two Sets

Next Stop Pittsburgh

WE WERE OFFERED TO PLAY for some of Pittsburg's Doo-Wop fans that September in 1999, but as Ilanga tried to explain to us during a rehearsal break about the call he received for this invitation it seemed interesting.

Ilanga could go into what I call a long winded explanation to anything when describing not only all the facts about a show offered to us, but every little detail that involved the gig itself.

Sometimes it was too much for me to endure as I stood there with the others waiting for him to finish speaking. Ilanga just wasn't getting to the point fast enough for me so I decided to interrupt him and raised my hand and said, "Who wants to go to Pittsburg?"

Everybody in the group put their hands up in agreement to what I was asking them. We just needed a simple yea or nay, nothing more complicated than that.

I always made sure that things were kept democratic with just about everything that involved the Band. The only difference was, this trip was pretty far from Boston, so we had to be sure that we really wanted to do it, but I needed a van. Next door where I worked was this Enterprise Car rental place. I knew the manager pretty well, and he gave me a great deal on a van, but he told me, "Mike, I'll give you the cheapest rate, but whatever you do, don't take the van out of Massachusetts."

"Yeah no problem," I said to him.

The next morning I picked everybody up and started that long "Fourteen" hour ride to Pittsburg. I wanted to do most of the driving. I didn't want to take any unnecessary chances by letting somebody else drive. It would have been difficult calling the rental manager to tell him something happened to the van while we were in Pittsburg. I'd rather be the one to take all the responsibility just in case something bad did go wrong.

Once we got to Pittsburg we settled into our hotel then made our way over to the show later that night. Again we gave a complete and successful performance for a very pleasant Doo-Wop crowd, and afterwards the promoter took us to one of those vintage theme restaurants called (Quaker Steak and Lube).

It had old hub-caps on the walls, part of the back end of a corvette sticking out of the wall with the rear tail lights on, a real car lift, old Texaco and Mobil sign's, photos of famous race car drivers, along with checkered flag's attached to the wall.

They wanted to show their appreciation for us coming all the way out to Pittsburg so I thought they treated us right. They just weren't music fans of Doo-Wop, they also showed that they had a lot of class to themselves as well.

The next morning I got up early and decided to take in some of the nearby local sights of Pittsburg before everybody else got up. They were all still in bed, and wouldn't be up for a couple of more hour's.

When I returned to the hotel, Payme and Teddy where in the parking lot waiting for me, and Payme looked pissed. As he started to cuss me out, Teddy told him to "Shut up". That put a stop to it. It was not how I wanted to start another 14 hour ride back to Boston, but it didn't matter, it still set the tone for the ride back home.

136 | Doo-Wop! and the G-Clefs: The Saga

THE BIGGEST "OLDIES BUT GOODIES" BOSTON CONCERT EVER

HARVEY ROBBINS' "ROYALTY OF DOO-WOPP©"
ARNIE "WOO WOO" GINSBURG'S FABULOUS 1950 & 60'S LIVE REUNION

ALL TOGETHER ON ONE STAGE...THE SHOW YOU'VE BEEN WAITING F

SYMPHONY HALL, BOSTON
FRIDAY NIGHT ~ FEB 25 ~ 8:00 -11:30 PM

IF YOU SAW THE PBS DOO-WOPP REVIVAL, YOU'LL GO WILD OVER THIS....EACH GROUP PERFORMS THEIR COMPLETE SHOW!!!!

e Grand Return on Stage
f All-time Radio Legend
ie Woo-Woo Ginsburg !!!

1) THE DRIFTERS
WITH SPECIAL GUEST
LOUIE LYMON
"Under the Boardwalk"
ve the Last Dance For Me"
"There Goes My Baby"

2) THE TOKENS
WITH ORIGINAL LEAD
JAY SIEGEL
"The Lion Sleeps Tonight"
"Tonight I Fell In Love"

3) SHIRLEY REEVES
ORIGINAL LEAD OF
THE SHIRELLES
"Will You Love Me Tomorrow"
"Soldier Boy!"
"Mama Said"

4) THE DEL VIKINGS
ORIGINAL
NORMAN WRIGHT
THEIR 1ST BOSTON SHOW
"Come Go With Me"
"Whispering Bells"

5) BILL HALEY'S COMETS
WITH LEGENDARY
AL RAPPA
"Rock Around the Clock"
"See You Later, Alligator"
"Shake, Rattle & Roll"

Call NOW
978-256-64

Harvey Robbins'
Productions

For Tickets
$36.50
$32.50
$26.50

THE G-CLEFS
BOSTON'S BELOVED
RIGINAL DOO-WOPPERS
"Ka Ding Dong"
"Cause You're Mine"
"Symbol of Love"

) LITTLE JOE COOK
RIGINAL LEAD OF THE

8) AND SO MUCH MORE !!!!!!

Symphony Hall

I'VE ONLY BEEN SCARED TWICE during my career as a musician, once when I was about to go on stage to play for at a small time bar in Waltham called the "Rendezvous". I remember one of my knees wouldn't stop trembling. The other one would be on February 28th, 2000, were I would repeat those same jitters of just being nervous while I was standing backstage ready to go on at Boston's "crown jewel" and most famous concert hall, Symphony Hall.

Waiting backstage at Symphony Hall – Boston 2000.

Although I had plenty of experience with all the years of playing on different stage's for all kinds of audience's doing gigs anywhere, and everywhere, so I don't know why this would feel any different for me, but for some uncontrollable reason it did.

I was more scared than nervous only for the fact that I understood the significance of playing at such a legendary landmark like Symphony Hall. It certainly has a long and prestigious history to it for the past 100 years of its existence. Maybe I was conscientious of that fact and wanted to pay it the respect I thought it required just to have the privilege of standing on its stage.

Years ago both sides of my family immigrated to this part of the country. One of my grandfathers (Irish), and a WWI veteran was also a Commander with his American Legion Post #156. He would be out front with a baton leading their marching band down Main Street on Veteran's day parades on the 4th of July. My other grandfather (French Canadian) played "Jigs" on the violin, but he was better at it on the piano when he sat down to play after work for his buddies in one of the many bars that existed on Main Street in Waltham.

I'm sure they would have been somewhat impressed and proud that one of their grandson's would have an opportunity to play at this superb acoustical concert hall that allowed only the best to grace its stage as it now allowed me to do so.

As I'm sitting in our dressing room there was that distinct smell of "refer" again. I knew what it was, but now there was also a noticeable cloud coming from the men's room around the corner. It was like the G-Clefs had fumigated the one and only place they felt free to occupy that seemed to be a safe haven for them to go and "lite-up". They always liked to smoke some marijuana before they went out on stage, and this show would receive a treatment no different than any other show they previously had done throughout their entire career.

When we finally got on stage we completely opened ourselves up and just floored it. Once again we were just right on. Everything went perfect, and as they say in show business, we really brought the house down. There were hands full of people dancing with each other in the isles along with cheers of approval to what our Rock 'n roll group provided that night in conjunction with what this Doo-Wop/Oldies show had demanded of us performers.

We always had high expectations for ourselves as a group, and this was where I thought we showcased our true talent that we developed from the constant gigs and the hard work we always injected into our rehearsals!

After the show was over and the music hall had emptied out, Bill and I, went back out onto that Stage. The lights were still shining brightly illuminating the hall. The work crews were breaking down the seats and sweeping the floor. Bill put his arm over my shoulder, and said, "...this is surreal Mike, I can't believe we actually played Symphony Hall!"

"Yeah Bill," I said to him, "I consider it a real honor for all of us."

I reflected for a moment, and said, "C'mon let's get outta here."

I didn't know it at the time, but Bill would tell me later he played our biggest show while suffering a concussion he received the night before playing in an ice hockey game, one of the roughest contact sport's out there.

Bill's hockey team had a game the night before and while he was waiting for one of his teammate's to pass him the "puck" in front of the opponent's goal crease, Bill got a full body check by an opposing player. He was knocked straight backwards hitting his head on the steel crossbar before he collapsed to the ice. Even though Bill was wearing a helmet but the force to his head knocked him out cold.

After leaving Symphony Hall that night, I had time to reflect with what we just finished doing as a group. It was a real personal achievement and a very long way to have come for all of us. It seemed as hard as any journey could be with the ups and downs that were everywhere we turned, but someway somehow we persevered to eventually play at one of the world's top concert hall.

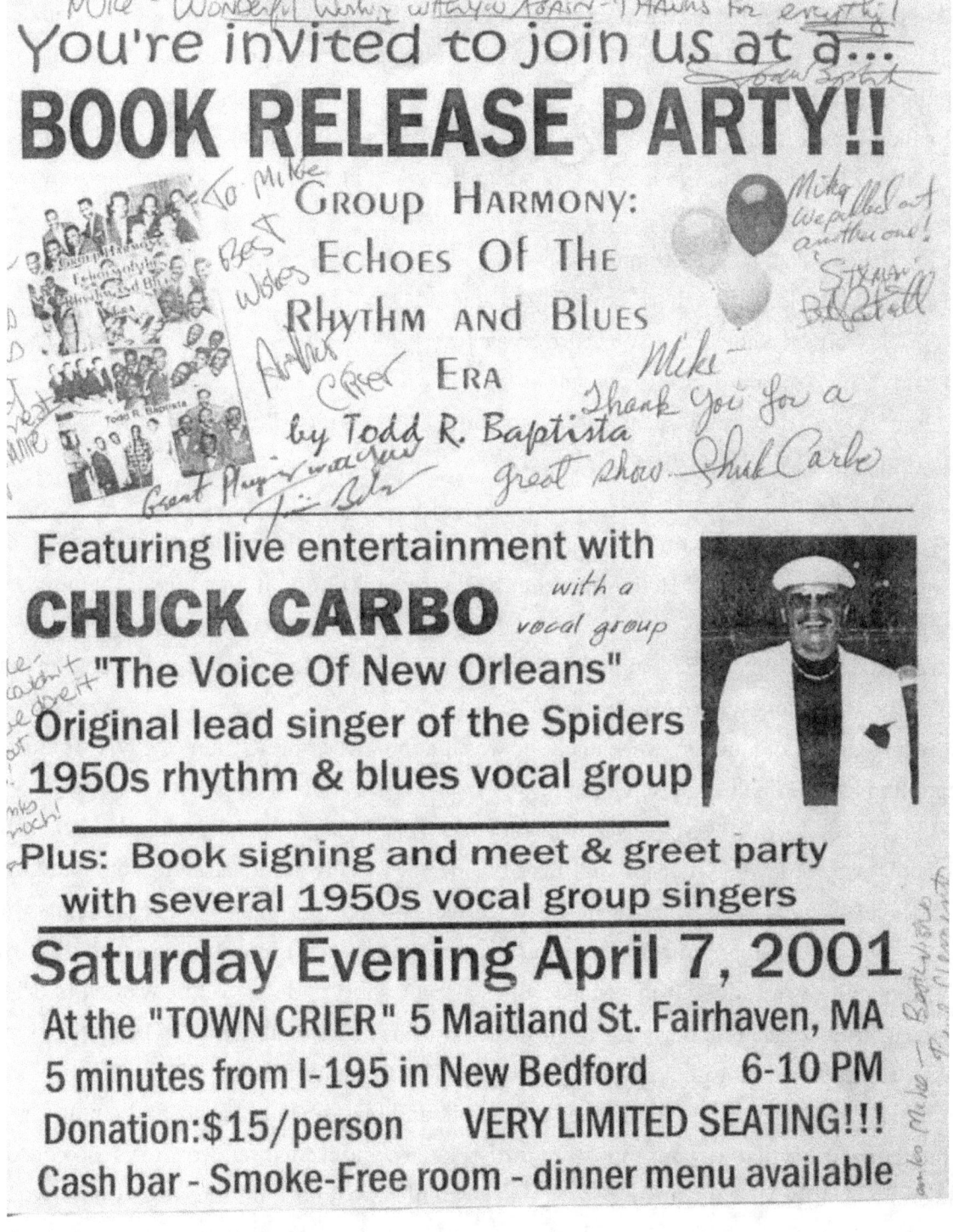

Chuck Carbo

AFTER THE NEW YEAR HAD ARRIVED, I received a call from Todd Baptista for another show he was promoting. He wanted me to put together a back-up band for a singer named Chuck Carbo, from the Spider's. This show would be at the VFW hall in Fairhaven, Massachusetts on April 7th, 2001.

I called Chuck Carbo at his home down in New Orleans, Louisiana, and introduced myself to him. I said, "... Todd gave me your set list of songs he would like for you to sing at the show here in Massachusetts."

Chuck then asked me, "How many set's did Todd want me to sing."

I said, "Well it looks like there's two full set's here."

"Oh," he replied, "how many songs are on each set?"

I said, "There's about 15 songs per set."

"Oh no, I can't do two full set's like that anymore," he told me. "I'm too old now."

I grinned and asked him, "How old are you?"

He said, "I'm 76."

"Yeah," I said, "I'll have you do just one set. We'll condense it down to one full set if that's okay with you, we won't tell Todd." He told me that he'll stretch it out a bit on some of the number's to make up the difference.

"Yeah okay," I said, "...that's fine. I wouldn't worry about it too much, I'm looking forward to meeting you when you get here Mr. Carbo."

My impression of him just over the phone was that he was genuinely a nice guy. I would not be disappointed when I finally got to meet him.

Since I needed to put together a backup band for Chuck, I thought I'd ask my band, the Bluesbirds, but they all backed down except for Bill. Like I said, Bill was always loyal and understanding, but sometimes it would give him what I call this carte-blanche to experiment with anything he wanted to try out. Bill and I had argument after argument on almost everything. If it was hiring his roadie which I thought was an added experience to Bill's already short budget, or if he wanted to bring his new 'lectric drum kit that he never tried out before for this gig. I wanted him to bring the standard acoustic drums for the show, but he wasn't going to listen to what I asked of him.

I hired some other top pro musicians to come in and play keyboards, sax and guitar for me. A little more expensive that way but they were professional's and it was well worth it. I also needed to fill the empty slot for back up singer's to do the harmonies we'll need on the songs Chuck would be singing that night. The only ones I could think of were the G-Clefs themselves.

I called Ilanga and told him I needed the G-Clefs to sing back-up for Chuck's gig. I wasn't sure if they were available, but Ilanga called me a couple of days later, and said they were more than happy to sing backup vocals on the show.

When Chuck finally arrived for his show, I noticed he was extremely nervous about being here. He told me that it had been years since he played out plus he said we were a band that he never worked with before.

I assured him everything would be fine, and not to worry. I made it a point to hang around with him before the show just to make him feel a little more at home. I think I was more nervous than he was. It all came together that night as the audience overwhelmingly loved Chuck's performance.

Those back-up musicians I hired held it together, and the G-Clefs did great singing back-up harmonies for him.

Last Gig

ONE MORE SHOW IN MANSFIELD with our yearly Barry Price gig for October, 2001 opening up for Ruth Brown, but this would be our drummer Bill's last gig with us. He had enough of the G-Clefs and decided to quit.

It could not have come at the most inopportune time for us, but there was nothing I could say or do to change his mind with this ill-timed decision of his. We still had three shows left to play before the year was out, and December was coming up with three Christmas parties we were already committed to play.

I tried to talk Bill into sticking it out for two more months, but nothing doing. He was done with the group, and was staying with his decision to leave. He said he had enough and couldn't take the G-Clefs anymore!

It was obvious he was not into doing this last show with us either. We all knew he couldn't wait for the show to be over with that night so he could finally break away from the G-Clefs once and for all, believing that he could walk away from the constant chaos you automatically inherited when you belonged to this band.

I certainly understood his reason for him leaving, but it would be difficult not having him stay for the remainder of the year. He certainly knew all of our songs inside and out.

It was going to be difficult to bring in another drummer that didn't know the material on such a short notice and try to get him up to speed so that he was somewhat proficient enough. All I could was hope for the best with whoever was available to come in and play drums for the remainder of our shows.

Me and Bill at one of Shorty's house parties – Cambridge.

This was one of the more difficult time's for me as there ever was. Although there were lots of tough episodes throughout the course of being with the G-Clefs, but I was hoping that we could get through these last three gigs in one piece before the year came to a close.

When December finally got here I would go through three different drummers in one month with the remainder of our gigs.

Unfortunately those drummers I hired weren't that good for various reasons but I can't really fault them. They came in, and did the best they could, and under the circumstances, I was more grateful than not.

When January finally rolled around, I was somewhat relieved that it was the beginning of a new year only because we had nothing coming up until spring time. I felt I could finally get some rest from this latest bizarre episode, or so I thought. All I really wanted to do was catch my breath and take a well-deserved break, but it would be short lived.

Coming Around Full Circle

WHEN 2002 FINALLY ARRIVED, it was already early winter when I received a phone call from Ilanga, "Mike, I have great news," he said, "I just received the contract from Harvey Robbins (the same promoter who booked us on our first show at Symphony Hall). He booked us again for a return date back at Symphony Hall."

"Oh that's great," I said, "Who else is on the 'bill' with us?"

"Oh no," said Ilanga, "nobody this time, we're the headliner's for this show. There might be one other band, but that's it."

"Oh yeah," I said, "I'm not surprised considering how well we went over on the first show," Ilanga continued to tell me, "...no, there'll just be one supporting act to open the show for us.

I said, "Oh great, okay."

I was happy with the thought of going back to play Symphony Hall. I also thought all the hard work finally paid off for us to have a top billing this time, and a nice pay day to go along with it, or so I thought. Ilanga suggested that I come over to his house for diner to discuss the new contract that Harvey had sent him.

"Alright," I said, I saw no harm with what he was asking. "What time do you want me to come over Ilanga?"

"Oh how about six o'clock tomorrow night," "he suggested, "we'll have dinner, and discuss the show."

"Okay," I said, "I'll see you tomorrow night."

When I hung up the phone I thought that's a bit strange. We always discussed anything that had to do with all of us as a group together not separately whether It's at our rehearsals, or band meetings at Teddy's house. We always took care of business with everybody there, and besides we never agreed to anything unless everybody took a vote on it. That was the way we always did it from the beginning. There was always a democratic stance to everything we did.

We all had to make sure everybody agreed with any show we were asked to do, and not have one person making decisions that concerned everybody else.

When I got to Ilanga's house the following night he seemed to be very excited about our return to Symphony Hall. We were very successful our first time there, and now it seemed that we were back in demand for a repeat performance. Things like that are normal in this business, so at the time I thought nothing of it.

"Wow," said Ilanga, "this is gonna be great, yes, back at Symphony Hall, for sure!"

Before I could say anything, Ilanga handed me the contract and said, "Mike sit down at the kitchen table here, and read the contract that Harvey sent me."

Right away I noticed it was already signed. It had Ilanga's signature on it. I said, "Ilanga, it's already signed by you, did you already agree to the terms? I hope you're not going to send it back to Harvey, we have to discuss this first."

"Oh yes," he said, "this is our copy."

I said, "Don't you remember? We all said not to sign anything until we all agreed to any contract no matter who it's from. Besides Ilanga, it says here that Harvey is to pay us $1,500 for the show. I thought you said that we were the top headlining act."

"Oh yeah, we still are," he said as I tried to remind him of our position as frontrunner on this show.

I immediately thought to myself for a headlining act on a show this big, we're getting low balled with the payment. This was not adding up in my head so I quickly reached over, and grabbed a paper napkin and a pencil.

As I started to scribble numbers on a paper napkin, "Listen," I said, "there are 2,632 seats at this hall. The average ticket for the show is $50.00. Hold on let me finish," I said as Ilanga tried to interrupt. I continued to multiply the figures and said, "Okay, look here, that's 130,000 dollars Ilanga. Are you kidding me, and you already agreed for all of us as a group to do the show for $1,500."

Immediately defending himself, Ilanga said, "That's the price we already agreed to with Harvey."

I said, "Ilanga, all of us are supposed to agree to a gig that involves us. Nobody can speak for everybody else. We're all supposed to take a vote, that's the way it's always been."

I was begging to understand why Payme would get upset with the other G-Clefs now.

I told Ilanga to "get Harvey on the phone. I'll talk to him if I have to. He can add on another "Zero" to that figure. He can at least give us $15,000 for the show. It won't be that much of a problem for him."

"Oh no, we can't do that," said Ilanga, "the tickets are already printed, and the show is sold out, and besides we've already signed the contract."

"You know Ilanga," I said, "even after Harvey pays for the rental of the hall, the insurance, the police, the union guys, and the tax's, he still walks away with at least $50,000 dollar's in his pocket."

This was my last attempt for Ilanga to listen to me and to be reasonable but I was getting too upset at this point and I knew my guys in the band would not be happy about it either. We were very conscientious not to have another big opportunity slip away from us, and it seemed that this one was about to be given away at our expense.

I got up from the table and left Ilanga's apartment. I never had a confrontation with him like this before and it shook me to the core, but I really felt I needed to stand my ground with him. To me it was a matter of good business, not to be taken totally advantage of like that. I didn't understand what he was thinking and why we were left out of the discussion process that involved that amount of money.

I was now suspicious and when I got home I started putting the pieces together in my head, but it still wasn't going to come out in my favor no matter how I tried to rationalize it.

I thought there might be a separate contract already agreed upon between Harvey Robbins, and the G-Clefs, and that I never got to see that "original" contract.

$1,500 dollars was our starting fee for any one of our performances whether it was for birthday parties or a wedding. Even after a big show back at Symphony Hall my band would only get paid $100 each playing in front of thousands of people that paid good money to see us. We got that much for playing some kid's bar mitzvah party in his parent's backyard, and even then we were back home by nine o'clock!

Two days had gone by when I left Ilanga's apartment, and that's when I received a phone call from him.

"Oh hi Ilanga," I said. "What's up?" I was a little more on the calm side this time. I immediately figured that he thought about what I said, and called the promoter to have the contract re-adjusted on what would be fair payment for our performance.

"Listen," as he started to say, then paused and said, "we decided that your services are no longer needed by the G-Clefs, and its organization. It will be best to go our separate ways."

Wow I thought that's low, but it didn't matter now. It was time to get off of this roller coaster ride that the G-Clefs offered me a while back, and for good. I certainly had had enough, and I knew I was exhausted with it all.

Even though I got to stand at the threshold to some small stardom that graciously came my way, "what goes around" eventually "comes around" as it now did for me.

Invite is not Optional

YEARS LATER AND WITH TIME having allowed me to move on from the G-Clefs, I would be cordially invited as a guest to Payme's surprise 70th birthday party in August 2008.

I was glad to get a call from Georgette, Payme's wife; she wanted me to be there, along with friends and family members. When I arrived, I was welcomed with open arms, not by all, but by most. That was the last time the G-Clefs and I spent any amount of time together. It was more of an informal get together a bit more relaxing with no pressure of getting ready to do a show for a waiting audience somewhere.

By now the G-Clefs were a bit older but I could see they were still the same people I got to know when I first started working for them. All in all I thought it was nice to be around them again.

There was none of that reminiscing about our time together, but that was okay with me. Besides, I didn't think we would get through any part of our previous journey as we struggled to become one in unison with a shared common goal; to make the best music we could.

During the party Abby, Dick's wife, said to me in our short conversation, "...Mike, I know the G-Clefs treated you badly..."

That was the first time I heard that kind of remark from somebody else associated with this group, but I also thought what she said held some truth to it. I reminded myself it's not what they did to me; it's what they did to themselves. I was merely there to help push their music along as best as I could, adding as much to it as I possibly could, only for others to take credit.

All in all it would be another eye opener as it removed any doubt about me playing this kind of music when its true magic would be heard again through the G-Clefs and any other singing group that started this music called "rock 'n roll".

The spotlight shined on all of them as another promise of Doo-Wop was played in our small corner of the world when it seemed to belong to the G-Clefs alone.

Mike Devlin

Special Feature!

Doo-Wop and The G-Clefs
In Their Own Words

By Michael G. Devlin

Doo-Wop and The G-Clefs—In Their Own Words

The G-Clefs

In Their Own Words

AFTER THE SCOTT FAMILY MOVED into their Roxbury home in 1944, a family named Gipson from Roberta, Georgia, purchased a house next door.

"See, we lived on Madison," said Ray Gipson. "They lived at #2, and, I lived at #4. We've been together ever since we were 5."

The Scott brothers Teddy, Chris, Tim, known later as "Payme", and Arnold who would change his name to "Ilanga" (pronounced "e-long-gah") made the G-Clefs a family affair.

Childhood friend Ray Gipson shared the stage with the siblings from the beginning. Joe Jordan, the Scotts' cousin, was a founding member, but would be drafted into the Army in 1957.

The five met while singing in the choir at St. Richard's, a catholic church where they learned the art of harmonizing, when they were in their early teens. Their activities outside of school became somewhat less angelic.

Ray Gipson

Between a steady stream of neighborhood chums and frequent house guests, the Scott household bustled with activity. "It was a great time," marveled group leader Teddy. "Our house was always loaded with kids, I don't know how our parents did it, because we only lived in a four room apartment."

Their parents stirred the brothers' earliest musical memories. "Our mother used to sing a lot," said Teddy, "before she got married. She was a second grade music teacher in Harwich, Ma."

Roxbury makes up that part of Boston known as the ghetto in the 60s and the inner city today, but the Scotts grew up during the 40s and 50s. Times were different; "it was ethnically and racially mixed," Teddy said. "We never thought of it as Roxbury the ghetto. It was totally mixed Irish, Italian, Chinese, Portuguese, Blacks. Totally integrated.

"Everybody," Teddy explained, "took care of one another. As kids, we sang on the stoop the doorstep. We could be out here till midnight in the summertime, and our parents wouldn't worry." That era was rich in all the good that family, friends, church and neighborhood provided; what lacked in the abundance of consumer goods that deluge society today. "Nobody had a television set," Teddy pointed out. "There was a TV store on the corner, so when there was a Joe Louis fight the sidewalks would be filled."

Teddy Scott

Gipson's parents, Albert and Corrine Gipson, introduced their son to music. "My dad played guitar," he said, "my mom's got a nice voice." Every Friday night four friends of his would come to the house and do a jam session. They would just play music and drink beer the whole weekend. Sunday night, it would all come to an end. They'd go back to work.

Chris Scott

If the Scott brothers found their personal sustenance and happiness at home and in the neighborhood, then they discovered their musical inspiration at church, as members of the boys' choir at St. Richard's catholic church. The brothers credit Father Tom Noonan, the choir director, with building their vocal foundation. "He taught us a lot," said Teddy. "We were a unique choir. Our choir was a mixture of religious hymns along with popular songs that were religious, like 'Lady of Fatima' and 'You'll Never Walk Alone'.

"He taught us to harmonize. We used to do those counterpoint melodies, like on the song 'I Understand'. Father Noonan taught us all that. We learned very much from him with people singing different parts at the same time. That was a very well-directed choir, and he would use diverse material, Irish songs, negro history songs, classical songs from Broadway shows, hymns in Latin and in English. A lot of our harmonies stem from the diversity which he had. The G-Clefs sound is really from the diverse material he had in the choir."

As much as the Scotts and Gipson enjoyed music, they hardly expected to earn a living at it. The vocal group that would become the G-Clefs got together in 1952—The Ink Spots, the Mills Brothers, and the Ravens. Teddy said, identifying early influences, "As far as black groups that were influential, they were the ones. There were lots of black gospel groups, but we weren't involved with that. We did all the pop songs."

In the original vocal lineup, Teddy sang baritone, and some alto. Chris sang second tenor, Tim sang baritone and bass. Joe Jordan sang bass, and Ray Gipson sang alto and first tenor. "Mainly," said Gipson, "I did leads, because I could not do harmony."

Payme (Tim) said, "You're the worst harmonizer in the world, but you can take care of the lead. I think the combination is with my brothers, the Scotts. They've got the northern pure sound, and here I come with the bottom of the barrel, very gutty soulful sound. And wow! We put the two together, and it worked. Tim, the only regular instrumentalist in the group, initially played guild and harmony acoustic guitars."

Initially, they called themselves the Bob-O-Links. "At that time," Chris observed, "groups were named after birds—the Wrens, the Flamingos, the Orioles, the Ravens, the Robins—then it moved on to music signatures—the Clefs, the Sharps the Flats, the Five keys. The quintet's name soon became the Clefs, until..." said Chris, "we found out there was a group recording as the Clefs. So we had to change our name. Our mother said, 'You sing "Gee" by the Crows all the time.' "

Tim "Payme" Scott

Taking Mrs. Scott's suggestion the group settled on the G-Clefs— "it was a signature in music, but we didn't realize it ourselves at that time," Chris said, "being a music teacher, our mother knew it."

So it stuck.

"We were singing at all the dances and picnics," said Teddy. "We rehearsed every single day in the living room of our house." In the years between 1953 and 1956 they ran their own dances. Their first gig, was at the Rollerway, a roller skating rink in Revere.

The young singers' entrepreneurial spirit led them to "promote other dances and shows every Friday night," said Teddy. "We'd rent the Ritz Plaza or Otis Field Hall or Butlers Hall or the Masonic Temple Hall for 50 bucks, and charge 75 cents admission. We ran dances everywhere, down the Cape, or the Roseland Ballroom in Taunton—everywhere. We were very industrious guys."

"Tuggles Hall was very important," Teddy explained, "because that's where we saw other acts— the Five Keys, the Drifters, Chuck Berry, Little Richard. All the early rhythm & blues acts would come and play there at Friday night dances. That's when the G-Clefs said, 'we're going to be like the Five Keys'. We were 15 or 16 years old, the Five Keys inspired us."

Arnold "Ilanga" Scott

Far from the only vocal group around the G-Clefs faced lots of competition. "Every block had a singing group," said Teddy. "They would try to out-do one another on opposite sides of the street." Among the local acts were the Dappers, the Love Notes, the Sophomores, the C-Quins, the Vibratones, the Majestics, and the Shields. Every block also had its own gang, in an era when gangs meant drinking, rivalries, and fist fights. The G-Clefs gang was known as the Victors. Their rivals were the Pythons, the Mustangs, the Shamrocks or the Red Raiders. Every gang had its turf and its colors. The G-Clefs speak about those days with relish but are quick to point out that it was a different time.

One of the gang members, Kevin Paulsen, frequently played guitar for the G-Clefs. In the year 1956, Kevin made the connection that changed the G-Clefs lives. "Kevin was backing up Pat O'Day at Ace Recording studio," said Teddy. "She was a big local talent who was doing 'Dear John'.

"Jack Gold, a native of Chelsea, was producing that session. He had a record with him that had been put out by the Rainbows on the Robin Label, but had not been widely distributed. Jack Gold asked Kevin if there was anybody around who could learn a song like "Mary Lee"? Kevin said 'Our group has been singing that song for years.' Gold didn't believe it. But, we had the record because of Audrey, one of the girls in our gang who had moved to New York."

Teddy continued, "She'd come and visit and would always bring us new rhythm & blues records, so we had the edge on all of Boston, all the later songs of the Orioles, Five Keys, Rainbows, Hank Ballard, Meadowlarks. Nobody ever heard of them in Boston. We had been singing 'Mary Lee' for three years because it was an exciting song."

"Kevin got on the phone and called us over to Ace Recording studio. We went up there and did it, and bang, we were cutting a demo record. That same night it was played on WBZ and WCOP, Boston radio stations. Jack Gold took it back to New York, but problems kept it from being released. Jack Gold had demos played on various radio stations and worked out a deal with Cecil Steen, owner of Pilgrim Records for which Gold was their A&R man, and sales manager."

The G-Clefs soon followed the path of every hopeful group of that era, and "cut a demo" at the hallowed Ace Recording studios. Ace turned out to be for the G-Clefs what Sam Phillips studio, Sun Records was to Elvis Presley. It wasn't state of the art sound quality, but it worked.

As they continued to improve, the G-Clefs began to receive a good deal of local attention by playing clubs such as Frankie Mack's at Revere Beach. It was while performing at that particular club that they came to the attention of Bill Marlowe, a legendary disc jockey and radio personality who was considered a mover and a shaker in the local music scene. "He took us under his wing," Payme remembered.

The record was getting a good deal of airplay, especially from their friend Marlowe, who played that song many times for three straight days. "The record made a lot of noise," said Payme. In the music industry parlance, signifying "a good deal of attention".

"Jack Gold said 'come up with another song'," Teddy noted, "and that's where 'Ka Ding Dong' came from."

Tim added, "It was as simple as that, a three chord progression." They'd been singing it since its initial recording in 1953 in a small studio in Malden.

Jack Gold listened to several G-Clef compositions, and he picked out 'Ka Ding Dong', "the one we hated," said Chris, "he picked the one we hated…"

Teddy quipped, "he always picked the one we hated."

That banter expressed the G-Clefs desire to sing rhythm & blues, an aspiration often frustrated by Gold who preferred pop tunes. "This was a new venture for him this rhythm & blues thing," stressed Chris.

Teddy added, "He had all white acts. He liked our sound because it didn't sound rhythm & blues. Even when we sang rhythm & blues songs, he could hear in his head that he could make us cross over."

Gold produced the up-tempo Doo-Wop number "Ka Ding Dong" at Ace Recording studio in

Park Square, Boston . "For Boston it was the studio," said Teddy. "In those days, it was the only big studio, it was small, but for Boston , it was big. It only cost us $150 to record the song."

The whole session was improved. The drummer had just a bass drum, a snare, and a cowbell—that's where the "ding dong" came from on the record. But he didn't even have a stand for the cowbell. He rested it on the bass drum, so he couldn't get any resonance out of it.

The G-Clefs promoted that disc at Boston radio stations—they visited Arnie Ginsberg at WBOX, Dave Maynard, and Bill Marlowe at WBZ, Joe Smith at WVDA, Jack Clayton at WHDH, and Jack Chartterton and Jack McDermott at WLYN in Lynn. " 'Ka Ding Dong' broke in Boston first," said Teddy, "because we'd go to all the stations every night, drink coffee and just hang around. It was all open to the disc jockeys then."

"Of course you had to do their record hops on the weekends, that was part of the program at that time," said Chris, "they didn't have program directors. The disc Jockey could play what he wanted to."

Many DJ's exacted a price for their cooperation. The G-Clefs paid managerial fees to several Boston disc jockeys and they shared song writing credit with one Jack McDermott. "We did that with 'Ka Ding Dong'," said Teddy. "Jack McDermott's name was on there. Jack McDermott still gets 50 percent writer's royalty, we learned. Still, nothing matched the thrill of hearing your song on the radio."

Released in June 1956, the record started taking off, along with the career of the G-Clefs. On September 1, 1956, "Ka-Ding-Dong" was rated a "Best Buy" in the industry, because it was doing well in so many regional markets: Buffalo, Boston, Cleveland, Detroit, New York, Philadelphia, Pittsburgh, and St. Louis.

After breaking in Boston "Ka Ding Dong" hit nationally peaking at #24 in billboard, #17 in Cashbox and #9 on the rhythm & blues charts. The G-Clefs had the distinction of being the first Boston group to have a national hit. The up-tempo tune with the nonsensical title, and the Doo-Wop sound would catapult the group to national fame.

Two white groups, the Diamonds and the Hilltoppers, covered "Ka Ding Dong" and competed with the G-Clefs original version for sales and airplay. "We were angry that it was covered three weeks after our release," said Teddy, "because we felt it would hurt our sales, which it did. We thought they were stealing someone else's song, stealing a rhythm & blues group song and making it white, so they could play it on the white stations."

The record really took off. "The next thing we knew, we were being booked into the Apollo theatre in New York. We were even invited to be on American Bandstand by Dick Clark." The phenomenal success of "Ka Dings Dong", which climbed up the charts in that dizzying summer of 1956 brought the G-Clefs the stardom that eluded the vast majority of musical hopefuls who dreamed of making the big time. But with it came some of the heartbreak and disillusionment that was part of the harsh reality of the times.

There may have been glory, but for most young singers, naïve, and grateful just to have a recording contract, there was little in the way of money after deductions for studio time, record promotion distribution, and public relations. "We were taken advantage of," said Payme without elaboration, but a tinge of bitterness.

A lot of things have changed since that long-ago era of hula hoops, hound dogs, penny loafers, mouse trap shoes, and powder blue jeans. The ethics of the recording industry, then and now leave something to be desired.

The G-Clefs success merited recording sessions in New York City, where Teddy sang lead on the late 1956 single "Cause Your Mine". " 'Cause You're Mine' was recorded at Columbia studios," said Teddy. "Now we went to two tracks—that was big time."

On November 17, 1956 "Cause You're Mine" received another excellent review. The record did well but it wasn't a hit like "Ka Ding Dong".

"Jack Gold wanted us to be a crossover group because we didn't sound black," said Teddy, "we had a lot of songs that we wanted to do which were rhythm & blues, but they always had something that would cross over."

Outside the recording studio the G-Clefs stuck to their rhythm & blues and Doo-Wop roots "but stage shows were nothing like our recordings," said Teddy. "We went to Buffalo first. George Lorenz was the big disc jockey up in the Buffalo area. He had us up there to the Zanzibar Lounge for two weeks. The dressing room was down in the cellar, next to where they put the empty beer bottles. Most of the rock clubs were like that then," Teddy added. "We went to the Apollo. Boy were we petrified!"

In September, 1956 the G-Clefs were booked at the Apollo for a week. "You did 13 shows a day for seven days. But you only did two songs."

There were a dozen different acts on the show. The Flamingos, the El Dorados, the Stereos, Moms Manbley, the comic team Freddie and Flo, and probably a tap dancer, Clyde McPhatter was the headliner.

Backed by the Apollo house band, the G-Clefs took the stage and delivered their recording studio bewilderment. They were confounded by the 16-piece band and the unfamiliar arrangements. "We didn't even know what song the band was playing," said Chris. "They were waiting for us to come in, and we were standing there. We were so used to hearing just the guitar, that when the horns came in, we didn't know what was happening."

"We couldn't sing a note," Teddy elaborated. "We were so stage struck, for four days the fright was so bad we couldn't even move our feet, although we'd been doing it for years. Frank Schiffman came back to our dressing room and told us, after tonight's show, 'you guys go back to Boston. You just don't belong on this stage'. We were scared, and we were heartbroken. We were afraid to go on stage again. We went out there for the nine o'clock show and the first two rows were filed up with Boston, our mother, Ilanga, and all the kids from Boston, bang! We snapped right out of it. All of a sudden we became big stars at the Apollo."

The G-Clefs - 1956

The G-Clefs frequently appeared on the same bill as Lloyd Price. "The Drifters Lloyd Price was always with us back in those days," said Teddy. "We always played poker in the dressing rooms and in the hotels, and he always lost. He'd be the headliner all the time and he'd announce the shows, and he never called us the G-Clefs, he always called us the G-Clips. The group met Chuck Jackson at the

Rock & Roll lounge in Pittsburgh, he was the bar boy," said Teddy, "the one who was cleaning up the bottles and washing dishes was Chuck Jackson.

"We'd have Chuck come up on stage and sing during a set. He'd sing things like 'You Never Walk Alone' ", that Roy Hamilton kind of stuff. Then he went with the Del Vikings after that."

On November 30, 1956, the G-Clefs were back at the Apollo. Others on the bill that week were the Five Satins, the El Dorado's, Margie Day, and JoAnn Campbell.

In December 1956, Jack Gold announced that he started his own Paris Label. Since two of the Pilgrim acts, the G-Clefs and the Four Esquires, were under contract to him, he took them both to his new enterprise.

Their release was "Symbol of Love" on the Paris Label in November 1956, and it would be later ranked as "excellent" on February 23, 1957.

Closing out 1956 at the Brooklyn paramount the G-Clefs performed for eight days on Alan Freeds Christmas Rock and Roll show, which starred screaming Jay Hawkins, Shirley and Lee, the Moonglows, the Heartbeats Jessie Belvin and other acts.

On March 1, 1957, the G-Clefs were back at the Apollo, this time with Big Maybelle, Solomon Burke, and the Love Notes. Alan Freed called the G-Clefs the "Cinderella Boys", a reference to their "overnight" rise to fame.

In April, the G-Clefs became part of Alan Freed's Easter Show at the Brooklyn Paramount. Others on the bill were, the Cleftones, the Pearls, the Solitaires, The Del Vikings, the Cellos, the Harptones, Bo Diddley, Bobby Marchan, the Rosebuds, the Rhythm Jesters, Charlie Gracie, Buddy Knox, and Jimmy Bowen.

The G-Clefs continued to tour during 1957 on the strength of "Ka Ding Dong". Once they traveled too far—"we went as far as Uniontown, Pennsylvania, with a big rock & roll show," said Chris, "and we ran into trouble. We went in to buy black socks in an army/navy store. They wouldn't sell them to us."

"We don't have any black socks," the salesman told Teddy.

Were Teddy's eyes deceiving him. "They're right there," Teddy pointed.

"We don't have any," the salesman reiterated menacingly, as he reached for the gun rack. The G-Clefs reached the door, problem was the door pulled inwards. As the exiting G-Clefs pushed outward, fortunately they untangled themselves and got out before that salesman loaded and pulled the shotgun trigger.

From then on, Chris insisted, "we said 'no, we cancelled all shows down south.' We lost a lot of money, but I'd rather not have the money."

The G-Clefs witnessed other disturbing examples of racism, some restaurants refused to seat blacks, forcing them to take the food out. "That was the Baltimore experience," said Chris, "check out only, or, if you went to a diner, sit under the blue roof section of the diner."

"That's where the coloreds eat," Teddy remarked.

"We were from Roxbury and we'd been in a United Nations all our lives. We never knew what prejudice was. We got scared and said 'that's it, we're not going any further. We'll get hung, knowing how brash we are.' After that we said we ain't going down south," Chris stressed, " 'cause we'd get killed."

It was during the mid-50s that a concert promoter named Alan Freed who coined the phrase "Rock 'n Roll" created a series of concerts up and down the east coast at venues such as the Paramount and Apollo theaters in New York, the Howard in Washington, and the Boston arena. On these tours the G-Clefs had their earliest opportunity to reach a broad audience. Freed was the first person who co-mingled black and white audiences, recalled Harvey Robbins, president and founder of the Doo-Wop hall of fame of America. He used the Rock & Roll because it was more accessible to white audiences.

"The artists that we listened to were from Chicago, Detroit, down south," said Chris Scott. "When you heard us, it was a northern sound. That's why back in the early 50s, 60s audiences could hardly believe we were black."

Ilanga added, "Because we were from the north, our diction was different and we sounded white. Sometimes they published our records without even putting our pictures on it."

"With the pressures of racism, we decided to cancel the southern leg of its first national tour in 1957. We were playing in Uniontown, Pennsylvania, at the time when we decided to cancel our shows in the south," Chris said. "We was from up north, and we couldn't deal with the racial situation down south, from the Mason-Dixon line on down. We had white fellas in the band, of course, and they couldn't stay in the same hotels with us. Restaurants, you'd either have to go to the back door or get takeout. That kind of situation we wasn't use to."

Their next appearance at the Apollo came on August 23, 1957, when they were part of a Dr. Jive show, along with the Dells, the Paragons, the Cadillacs, the Cleftones, JoAnn Campbell, Johnnie & Joe, the Shells, Tommy Brown, and Pretty Boy (Don Covay)

LIFE ON THE ROAD

GEORGE LORENZ HAS BEEN SUFFICIENTLY impressed with the G-Clefs Zanzibar debut to ask them to be on a bill, headlined by Gene Vincent and his Blue Caps.

George Lorenz "was called the 'Hound Dog'," said Tim, "out of WKBW, Buffalo. He had a tour going up to Toronto down to Seattle, and back. Those were great shows, probably the most memorable shows because the audience appreciated you. That would be the youngest kids, when rock 'n roll was really getting big. At the Apollo you has an older, musically educated audience.

"There was quite a difference when you played a concert for kids who just wanted to see you. What a feeling for an artist, what a boost. Those were all good times, really positive times."

Meeting other musicians was a side benefit of touring. "We worked with Gene Vincent quite a bit," said Tim. "I got pretty friendly with his drummer, Dickie Harrell. We were on a tour for about three months, so we got pretty close."

The G-Clefs covered the chitin circuit, which stopped at urban theaters, attracting mostly black audiences. "You played the Brooklyn Paramount, the Apollo in New York City the Royal theater in Baltimore, then to the Howard in Washington, the Regal in Chicago, and the Uptown in Philadelphia," Chris said. "The whole show would travel. The tour appeared at a venue for one week then moved on to the next city. Sometimes, everyone rode in a touring bused, but not always. We had an old broken down car, it was an Oldsmobile, but we used to call it the 'Old-mobile'."

The G-Clefs often felt awed by other artists on the bill. "We had all those people's records at home," said Teddy. "We'd say 'oh my, we're with these groups. What am I doing here?' When we get as famous as them, we'll be able to buy a station wagon too."

"When I was really influenced by rhythm & blues," Chris recalled, "it was Clyde McPhatter, Jackie Wilson, the Drifters and Tommy Hunt who was with the Flamingo's.

"Folks like that who we used to work with at the Apollo or Howard Theater, you'd just stand back in the wings and watch them, and just be amazed. To me, us, being there was just some kind of dream that happened and I didn't even understand why, how, or where, except we were there.

"We happened to be lucky; we were blessed to be there."

Scott looks back at the years and remembers the ups and downs of those early days. He remembers watching Buddy Holly, the young rock and roll immortal, performing at the Apollo theater before an all-Black audience. "They loved him!" Scott exclaimed.

Chris said, "We shared one of the dressing rooms with him. In those days the Apollo use to lock us in because they were afraid of all the different performers coming and going, that they might leave the theater and not come back on time for their show."

"In the 50s I loved working with the Five Keys," said Tim, "They were our idols before we were famous. So, when we met them we looked up to them and they took us under their wing. They helped us out quite a bit in 55 and 56. We were young and the Five Keys were in their early 30s, so they looked out for us."

"They were a great group and they did a lot for us," agreed Gipson. "They were so polished, they were the Temptations of that era. When they walked on stage, you could hear a pin drop. They had an aura about them." Gipson remembered another influential performer, "His name was Nate Nelson. He was the lead singer for the Flamingos. I'd just stand in the wings and watch him. He was so smooth."

In the late 50s, the G-Clefs literally brought the house down, when they performed at a fundraiser at Mechanics building located in Boston on the site of the Prudential Center today. The show featured such national acts as Frankie Avalon, Chuck Berry, Dale Hawkins, and Dinah Washington, but the home town crowds exploded when the local boys took the stage. "People were jumping so hard for us the balcony fell," said Teddy.

In 1958, the G-Clefs stopped recording for four years. Although the group continued performing, Teddy remembered that "the members took turns being sent to jail." They felt they owed it to their fans not to record with that image, so they waited until the dust settled. In spite of these "youthful indiscretions," they all managed to finish high school during this period.

After changing record labels, the group sought to crossover to a wider market. The year was 1960 and a time of great changes not only in music but in society, culture and politics. America was stretching and yawning out of the Eisenhower years into the new frontier of the Kennedy administration. The G-Clefs found a song that they liked, written by Pat Best called "I Understand", which was a downbeat almost melancholy ballad about a lost love. A friend, Joe Jordan came up with the idea of mixing the G-Clef singing "Auld Lang Syne" into the background.

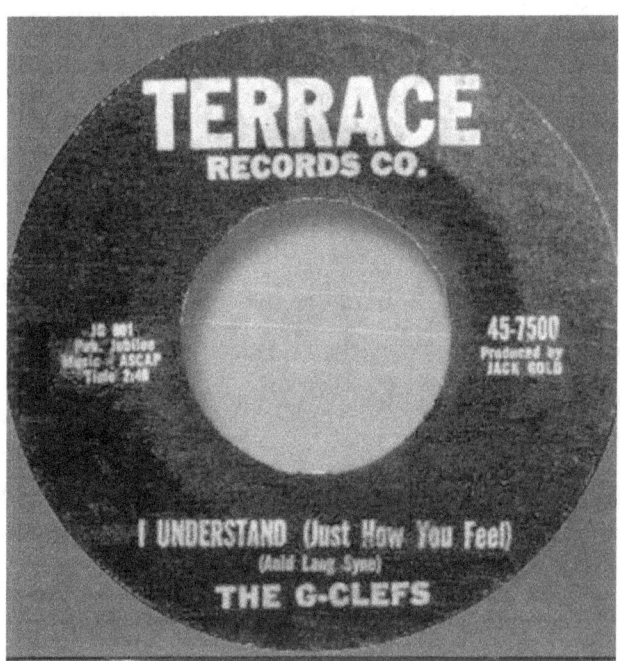

It was a stroke of genius. The record took off like John Glenn's rocket soaring high into space. It made music history charts in the summer of '61 and launching the G-Clefs on a tour of the US and Europe. The G-Clefs had several other hits including "Symbol of Love" and "Cause You're Mine" and an up-tempo semi-a cappella gem, written by Scott and his wife called "Make up your Mind", which many die hard G-Clef fans will recall as one of their very best recordings.

And he remembers touring the American south after "I Understand" boosted the G-Clefs into mainstream radio.

The G-Clefs had been booked to play at a religious school for girls. The head of the school met them and declared, "oh heavens no," and paid them and asked them to get back on the train without having sung a note. "I think that they thought we were a white act," Scott said bemusedly.

Unfortunately, incidents such as those were all too common during those heady days of America's awakening to the civil rights movement.

The G-Clefs continued to work up new song arrangements, in one case, Chris toyed with blending Auld Land Syne and another song, finally settling on "I Understand" composed by Pat Best. "I

Understand" had reached the top ten in 1954 for the pop vocal group the Four Tunes.

"I had put 'Auld Lang Syne' with a tune by the Orioles, 'What are you doing New Year's Eve'," said Chris. "I was just playing around with it thinking of putting it in there as a counterpoint in the background. But the fellows didn't like it, they didn't think it worked.

"So when we were doing a Four Tunes song, in my mind I was singing 'Auld Land Syne'. I said, 'let's put it in here.' And it became part of our repertoire."

" 'I Understand' was around the group for about six years before we recorded it," added Tim. "I love it by the Four Tunes. They harmonized a chime in the background, 'I understand, bong, just how you feel, bong'. Chris came up with the idea of 'Auld Lang Syne', that made it click."

In 1960, Jack Gold passed through Boston again. Teddy phoned Gold telling him that the G-Clefs had new songs. The group rendezvoused at Gold's room at the Hotel Touraine on the corner of Boylston and Tremont streets in Boston. "We went through a whole bunch of songs," said Chris. "Jack Gold said 'what else have you got?' I said we have 'I Understand'. When we sang it, he fell off the bed. He said that 'that's the one'. He was very excited, and that's the one he picked".

"We didn't think 'I Understand' would be anything," said llanga.

Chris interjected, "I was the only one who liked it because I had put the arrangement together. 'I Understand' fit nicely into the pop style that Gold favored. The payola scandal had changed the industry," said Chris. "Jack Gold told us they were going to blackball rhythm & blues on the main radio stations, and the main record companies weren't going to do more rhythm & blues recordings. That's why he liked 'I Understand' so much, because it crossed us right over from rhythm & blues."

Gold took the G-Clefs to A&R studios in New York. By this time they "had more tracks, more sophisticated equipment," said Chris, "music tracks and vocal tracks were separate, so if the tracks didn't come out right, then you could go back to New York next-week, and overdub."

"Teddy and I did the leads on 'I Understand'," said Ilanga, who was recording with the G-Clefs, for the first time. "Jack Gold liked that quality of sound between Teddy's voice and my voice. Those two leads singing the same melody, the same notes, we also did 'A Girl has to Know' and 'They'll Call Me Away' with those double leads."

"That sound was something Jack Gold discovered—he had some ear, an incredible ear", added Chris. "Jack Gold wanted to try that duet unison sound with the two leads singing against the background. We were the first to do that, and then a lot of groups started it after that. We didn't even sound like the G-Clefs then. It was a new G-Clefs, outside of Boston. Most folks thought we were white when 'I Understand' came out." Convinced he had a hit on his hands, Jack Gold hired Billy Mure to arrange and orchestrate the sessions. Gold proved exceptionally particular about these recordings; setting up separate booths for each singer, putting handkerchiefs in everyone's hands to prevent the reflexive hand clap or finger snap, and filling gaps between teeth with wax to avoid a hissed 's'.

"We were doing 'I Understand' when Ilanga's toe cracked," said Teddy.

"He moved back from the mic in the booth and his toe went 'crack'. Jack Gold screamed 'Who did that, what was that?' He went crazy," echoed Ilanga. "It was a great take, one of those great takes, and I moved my foot."

It was released on Terrace Records in late 60s with its "Auld Lang Syne" holiday hook. "I Understand" was released in August 1961. It failed to hit, even in Boston, but, during the summer of 1961, the record started to pick up radio play, and in September, it tracked the national charts. "I Understand" climbed to #9 on Billboard's Hot 100, and it clung to the charts through the end of 1961. The pop smash revitalized the group's career and the G-Clefs were at the Apollo again, on October 27, 1961. Ultimately performing at that venue for seven separate week-long appearances. The bill included Shep & the Limelites, the Stereos, the Spinners, The Orlons, Tommy Hun and Timi Yuro, and the Reuben Phillips Orchestra.

It must have been bittersweet watching Freddie and the Dreamers, a comic British beat group, crash the top 40 with the G-Clefs "Auld Lang Syne" arrangement of "I Understand" during March 1965.

The G-Clefs joined national tours again and again. They struck up friendships with acts they met on the road. "You never had a chance to go out of the theaters," said Teddy. "It was too dangerous, because of kids who wanted souvenirs and wise guys who'd mug you.

"You had dressing rooms in the theaters, so you stayed in the theaters all the time. You became family. You name 'em, and we've been with em'. Little Anthony, Mickey and Sylvia, the Impressions, and Curtis Mayfield taught us a lot of the chord structures that we use now. He taught us in the dressing rooms."

"Nor was that the first time that violins had compromised a G-Clefs song, that was a song Tim wrote," Chris said, "about 'Little Girl I Love You', the 'b' side of 'I Understand', that's like a cowboy song. Billy Mure was the arranger and he added violins, sounding like horses. He made it sound really country. We had it more rhythm 'n blues, and he added that country sound to it, and it really sounded country."

The G-Clefs had to locate other music on the AM dial because rhythm & blues had been limited to a couple of hours a day on Boston radio during their youth. "We used to listen to the radio and always be tuned to the Red Foley station," said Teddy.

Ray Gipson added, "We had no choice. It was either Patti Page or Gene Autry."

The country influence proved valuable when the group played at state fairs in the Midwest, where family audiences often favored country & western over rhythm & blues because "we were so crossover," Teddy said, "they didn't know we were black when they booked us. One Christmas eve, we played the Niagara Falls Theater, and we had to sing all country & western songs. Our big hit there was the flip side of 'I Understand', 'Little Girl I Love You'. They thought we were country and western artists. Good thing we had learned all the cowboy songs when we were kids."

In the fall of '62, Terrace Records issued "Sitting in the Moonlight/A Lovers Prayer", the third G-Clefs single of that year—the most discs the groups had ever released in one calendar year. The two songs featured string arrangements by Gary Sherman who had previously worked on the Drifters productions. The contrasting song styles, one urban rhythm & blues, the other a pop ballad, pointed to the musical differences separating the group and producer it was trying to feel that out and to work with that again. It was romantic. He was more into "A Lover's Prayer".

"Jack Gold wasn't keen on doing 'Moonlight'," Chris noted. "We wanted to do it. We kept pestering and pestering him to do it. So, he finally did it, but I don't think he was enthused about it."

"Sitting in the Moonlight" was written by Johnny Ray Rice, a friend of the G-Clefs. Rice had been in the Splendors, the group which included two Scott brothers, Ilanga and Ernie. "He wrote a lot of other songs, but we didn't use them," Teddy said regarding Rice. " 'Moonlight' was up-tempo in the Drifter style, with those strings running. It was a nice tune."

"A lot of other people 'died' at certain times," said Gipson, "like when the Beatles came in. Oh baby, it was hard to get work if you didn't have a Beatle haircut and four guitars. The money went down because all they were buying was Beatlemania. It made it tough."

As the G-Clefs record sales and radio play cooled, their live shows heated up. "We became G-Clefs incorporated," said Teddy. "We realized the only way we were going to make any money as the G-Clefs was to own it all. We started doing that in 1963 or 1964 when personal appearances became very successful financially. As a corporation we didn't have to personally pay any bills at all—the corporation paid for clothing, instruments, air fares, hotel rooms. As part of the corporation, you got a salary. In those days we got $200 a week; that was a lot of money.

"It seemed like even more when contrasted with record royalties. We thought we were going to be millionaires right away," Teddy admitted. "Sell a million records, and we'd get a million bucks.

Nobody told us it was a cent and a half a record. And you had to pay for the sessions. We never got a royalty statement that we didn't owe them.

"Everybody assumed we were rich because we had hit records. Nobody realized we were still poor. Supposedly royalties come in every six months, but they don't, and when they do come, you owe them money for recording sessions."

Chris concurred, "We always owed them for the next session."

On the road in 1964, the G-Clefs were booked through Bob Walkers American program bureau, an agency that also arranged lectures. He took them to Jack LaForge's Regina label, were they changed to a soul sound.

Walker developed a college circuit that kept the G-Clefs playing dances and mixers at schools and fraternity houses, fifty two weeks a year. "We'd do anything that was on the radio. We rehearsed every day. We learned two or three songs a day and did them that night."

In addition to the bustling college circuit, the G-Clefs headlined nightclubs during the 60s, and early 70s. "You were at those clubs seven nights a week and you did four or five shows a night," said Teddy. "We could never remember all the clubs we did, because we did so many."

In New York City, the G-Clefs performed at the Copa, Rude Hellers, and the Peppermint Lounge. When nothing happened with any of their recordings at Regina, they returned to Jack Gold in 1965. By this time, Gold was an executive at United Artists and he got them a contract with UA's Veep subsidiary. They recorded two singles on Veep Records. Their first recordings with Veep were released in April 1965.

In the mid 60s radio tuned to Motown, American folk rock and the British invasion. In 1966 they left the Veep label, and had switched over to the Loma label, a subsidiary of Warner Brothers records.

In Revere, a beach front community on the Massachusetts coast, they packed Hurley's, the Beach Ball and the Ebb Tide, in Boston the Sugar Shack was one of the many rooms they filled. "We made Revere the nightclub city. Then other bands started coming up. The most fun I ever had was with the Chambers Brothers in the mid-60s," Chris recounted, "I love that group."

"We did a lot of work with them. We went in the promoting business ourselves, we booked ourselves and we booked the Chambers Brothers with us. That's how we really got to know them It was good chemistry—the audience liked our style and their sound. We worked with them at Hurley's and the Tiger Tail for a year in Revere—same two bands—and filled every night, sold out. We even owned our own club for a while on Revere Beach," said Teddy.

During 1967, the G-Clefs took over a club that played the name game, from Murphy's by the Sea to the Peppermint Lounge to the Tiger Tail. The G-Clefs called it the Pied Piper.

One night at the Pied Piper, members of an organized crime family approached the group. They asked why the G-Clefs "never played Las Vegas?"

"We told them the G-Clefs have always been an integrated group," said Teddy. "They wouldn't book us in Vegas unless we had an all-black band. In Vegas you had to be either all black or all white at that time, so we refused to do Vegas."

Only a few years earlier, the G-Clefs had been virtually run out of the south for being too black. Now Vegas judged them not black enough. Whatever that crime family's sins were prejudice was not among them. The G-Clefs suddenly received unexpected offers from Vegas clubs. By the summer of 1967, the group was headlining the Pussycat a Go Go, a hip nightspot that attracted a crowd ranging from NASA astronauts, to gangsters.

Leaving Las Vegas, the G-Clefs traveled to clubs in San Jose, Sacramento, and San Francisco. "At the Mars club in San Jose, we couldn't get our instruments out, the IRS locked the doors," said Teddy. After explanations to the IRS, and frantic phone calls between Boston and Washington, and the west coast, the G-Clefs managed to retrieve their equipment and predictably the check from the club never came.

During 1967 the G-Clefs recorded their first album at the beach ball in Revere. "The G-Clefs -Live" was a typical club performance, including "Ka Ding Dong", and contemporary hits like "Hold On, I'm Coming". Spotlight Records, a label co-owned by Teddy Scott, pressed about 2000 copies of "The G-Clefs - Live" for distribution at the group's dates.

The G-Clefs sojourned in Britain where "I Understand" had reached #17 in late '61, for club tours that lasted three months. They soon learned how the British club circuit differed from its American counterpart. American clubs booked acts for a least one full week of dates. British gigs lasted only one night at the most. "Sometimes we did two or three shows a night in different cities," said Teddy. "It was so hectic, a lot of times we just called and said 'the van broke down, we can't make it.' You'd go 300 miles one way, and then you'd have to come back 300 miles."

The G-Clefs got a temporary reprieve when they teamed with some of friends. "We ran into the Chamber Brothers in England," said Tim. "We had a ten city tour with them in Manchester, Liverpool, and London. They had a bus, so we went in their bus. We had a lot of fun.

They also encountered an American guitarist on the verge of super stardom. "We met Jimi Hendrix," noted Tim. "He came into our dressing room. He even picked up the guitar and started playing. It was strange. I didn't see him again until I went to catch him in America. I was very impressed. I went backstage and asked, 'do you remember me?' 'Of course,' he said. I was shocked, because now he was a giant."

During 1969 and 1970, the group played three month engagements at the Mugen, a dance club in Tokyo, Japan. "Japan was very excellent," said Ray Gipson. "We were treated like we were gods. We had limos, we had bodyguards. They couldn't do enough for us, and in return we gave them our best, musically, carrying ourselves as gentlemen and as entertainers. It was a great time for us."

"Another world altogether," agreed Chris. "We were like major stars there, because there were only two or three American artists over there. We were like the Temptations over here."

The G-Clefs, was the featured American act, headlined every night, often supported by a Japanese, or other Pacific band. "We worked with this group called Eva and the Esplanades," said Gipson. "They were out of the Philippines. They could go home and listen to a tune and come back the following night and play the thing to a T, they were excellent."

"There was a $75 cover charge to get in the door," said Teddy, "and after eight o'clock, you couldn't even get near the door. We played there every single day, and every day the nightclub changed the décor."

In Britain the G-Clefs changed clubs daily, in Japan the club changed around them. The G-Clefs sang at Expo '70 the Japanese World's Fair that booked such international stars as Frank Sinatra, Andy Williams, and Sammy Davis, Jr. Additionally, the group appeared weekly on a television program called "720".

The G-Clefs ran a tight organization that enforced strict rules regarding the stage clothing worn by the entire band. "We were well known for our wardrobe on stage," said llanga, who coordinated the groups outfits. "That was one of the joys of coming to see us, because the audience wouldn't know what we were going to be wearing. We had many, many outfits. It went from the 50s tuxedo era into the Go Go period, the English trend, the mod trend, the 60s. Flower power trip, the Sly Stone period with the frills and the buckskin and the fringes hanging down, but we always maintained the formal dress, like a tux even though we had outfits in all different styles."

If the elaborate wardrobe appealed to the audience, it tripped up band members tempted to break the dress code. The G-Clefs developed a system of fines for wardrobe infractions. Ilanga executed the penalties. They were fined if anything was out of line, "very high too," he said, "there was no fine under $25, even if your shoe wasn't shined. That was the only way it was maintained with 10 guys."

Ilanga, emphasized, "Ray Gipson, he was god—his law was it. He'd say 'this is what we're wearing', and that was it. He was wardrobe man. He was the fine man, and he was the collector man. He took care of everything, but the rest of the guys did their jobs, also. The G-Clefs always dressed to the max. We were the Temptations, as far as wardrobe goes."

The G-Clefs spiced their performances with comedy skits, perhaps inspired by the comedians from the Apollo shows. Or maybe the humor evolved naturally among brothers and friends whose repartee and rapport is still sharp today. "We made up shows," Teddy said. "We would design and make our own sets, and we'd do comedy routines of the dating game and shows like that. It became so big, people would come to see what show we were doing. We were so natural—the G-Clefs were very comical guys."

The G-Clefs avoided the music scene for more than a decade, although occasionally performing at oldies shows, or special events. They dropped the frenetic club schedule that had gone on night-after-night, when Discos substituted a single disc jockey for a multi piece band which caused the demise, from a financial perspective. But the group members also decided to pursue other avenues of life, college, jobs and families.

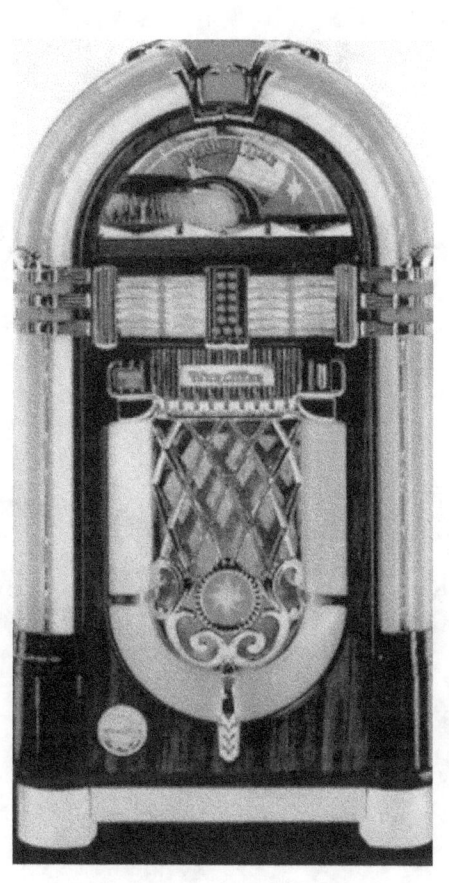

THE G - CLEFS

May 2000 – Discoveries – by Joseph Tortelli

About the Author

Born in Kentucky, Michael was six months old when he started traveling extensively as a young boy. His father had a career with the US Army for twenty years and moved constantly.

"We lived across most of the United States, and including Europe. I saw the world and learned to speak different languages. Once we got back to the states we lived in racially mixed neighborhoods. I think that allowed me to interact as well as I did with the musical community. They're a very diverse group of people, and I was able to fit in with them. People often ask my favorite places to live which are Barcelona, Spain, and Lawton, Oklahoma."

When his father retired from the army, the family moved back to Boston. Michael being uprooted most of his life was still able to start and finish high school within one school system. He graduated from college, worked as an expeditor, went to computer science school at night, then worked at MIT before getting into music. Interestingly enough Michael drove limousines transporting celebrities such as "Little Richard", Willie Nelson, Bruce Springsteen and the Beach Boys, plus many more high profile people.

"It worked out perfectly for me. There was a lot of down time with that job. It was there that I could really work on the manuscript for my book Doo-Wop and the G-Clefs."

Michael lives near Boston, Massachusetts where he still works and plays guitar.

Find these 2 books for digital readers on Amazon.com or Barnes and Noble Nookstore:

Michael G. Devlin's

Doo-Wop and The G-Clefs:

The Saga of America's Last Original Doo-Wop Group from the 1950s Still Performing

&

Michael G. Devlin's

Doo-Wop: and The G-Clefs In Their Own Words

www.ingramcontent.com/pod-product-compliance
Lightning Source LLC
LaVergne TN
LVHW081357060426
835510LV00016B/1877